Stuart Barlow is in the family team at Bhatia Best Solicitors. He has specialised in Family Law for over 40 years. His focus is now on representing Parents and other parties in Children Cases. He is a member of the Law Society Children Panel and Accredited Specialist with Resolution in Private Children and Cohabitation Law. He is the former Chief Assessor of the Law Society Family Law Panel and adjudicator for the Legal Aid Agency. He is a regular presenter of training courses for family lawyers throughout England and Wales and the author of several family law books.

Running a Family Law File – A Handbook for Trainees and Paralegals

Running a Family Law File – A Handbook for Trainees and Paralegals

Stuart Barlow

LLB (London) Solicitor

Law Brief Publishing

© Stuart Barlow

All rights reserved. No part of this publication may be reproduced, stored in a retrieval system, or transmitted, in any form or by any means, electronic, mechanical, photocopying, recording or otherwise, without the prior permission of the publisher.

Excerpts from judgments and statutes are Crown copyright. Any Crown Copyright material is reproduced with the permission of the Controller of OPSI and the King's Printer for Scotland. Some quotations may be licensed under the terms of the Open Government Licence (http://www.nationalarchives.gov.uk/doc/open-government-licence/version/3).

Cover image © iStockphoto.com/Andranik Hakobyan

The information in this book was believed to be correct at the time of writing. All content is for information purposes only and is not intended as legal advice. No liability is accepted by either the publisher or author for any errors or omissions (whether negligent or not) that it may contain. Professional advice should always be obtained before applying any information to particular circumstances.

Published 2023 by Law Brief Publishing, an imprint of Law Brief Publishing Ltd
30 The Parks
Minehead
Somerset
TA24 8BT

www.lawbriefpublishing.com

Paperback: 978-1-916698-04-8

This book is dedicated to my seven wonderful grandchildren: Bethany, Sam, Joseph, Rosie, Ava, Flynn and Halle for whom I am thankful

PREFACE

A group of students stood on the steps of the College of Law, Guildford. It was 1975. They were about to launch into a week of intense final examinations at Alexandra Palace in North London. They said their farewells to each other and shared their plans for the future. One student said to his friend: 'I see you as a family solicitor, for sure'. The friend saw himself as a criminal solicitor, but replied: 'Let's see what our Articles (training contract) brings'.

By the time his Articles had come to an end, the second student had arrived at a decision about his future career. Criminal and Family Law were for him and for many years he practised both. In the end, Family Law won the day and has done for the last 25 years of his legal career. I have never regretted it!

I have had the immense privilege of working with and learning from many family lawyers. I am thankful for those who have graciously corrected me (including members of the Judiciary) when I have gone wrong and encouraged me on the occasions when I have needed help. There are too many to list here and some will not even realise how good they have been to me. Many thanks to all of them.

Special thanks go to my wife, Sue, for her help in editing this book and correcting the mistakes in my grammar and style. Thanks to my friend, Joe Morgan, who has produced the graphics in this book. Also to MBL Seminars who enabled me to rehearse some of the contents of this book when teaching lawyers from all over England and Wales in their seminars. Finally, I thank Law Brief Publishing who supported me in the writing of this book.

The law and procedure is correct as of 1st June 2023.

Stuart Barlow
June 2023

CONTENTS

Introduction		1
PART A	FIRMS, FILES & CLIENTS	3
Chapter 1	The Structure of Law Firms	5
Chapter 2	Internal Workings of a Law Firm	9
Chapter 3	Roles in a Law Firm	13
Chapter 4	Information Ahead of the First Meeting	17
Chapter 5	The First Meeting With the Client	19
Chapter 6	Follow Up Work After the First Meeting	27
Chapter 7	Vulnerable Clients – Matters to Look Out For	29
Chapter 8	Managing Clients' Expectations	35
Chapter 9	Management of a Family Law File	39
Chapter 10	Funding a Family Law Case	51
Chapter 11	Closing a Family Law File	55

PART B	ORDERS	63
Chapter 12	Family Court Orders	65
Chapter 13	Divorce Proceedings	71
Chapter 14	Financial Applications	75
Chapter 15	Private Children Applications	81
Chapter 16	Public Law Children Applications	87
Chapter 17	Domestic Abuse Injunctions	93
Chapter 18	Other Family Proceedings	101
PART C	COURT	105
Chapter 19	Arriving at Court	107
Chapter 20	Inside the Court Room	109
Chapter 21	Different Tribunals	113
Chapter 22	Types of Hearings	117
Chapter 23	Evidence on Oath	121
Chapter 24	Remote Court Hearings	123

PART D	PROCEDURES	129
Chapter 25	Alternatives to Court Proceedings	131
Chapter 26	Drafting Applications and Statements	139
Chapter 27	Preparing Court Bundles	145
Chapter 28	Instructing Counsel	153
Chapter 29	Finding of Fact Hearings	161
Chapter 30	Cafcass and Local Authority Reports	171
Chapter 31	Litigants in Person & McKenzie Friends	183
Chapter 32	Instructing Experts	205
Chapter 33	Drafting Court Orders	217
Chapter 34	Appeals	223
Chapter 35	Enforcement of Court Orders	227
Chapter 36	Thirty-Three Common Questions Asked by Clients in Family Cases	233

INTRODUCTION

Practising family law is a rewarding occupation but it is not for the faint-hearted. Over and above the emotional and human aspects of the work, one of the biggest challenges is the fact that law and procedure in family law is constantly changing. Family law is immensely wide-ranging and no individual area has escaped some kind of statuary or procedural change: divorce has moved from fault to no fault; children law has transitioned in stages from the vague and general to being highly sophisticated statute and case law based; domestic abuse, once tolerated as a way of life, is now subject to intense protection and is a criminal offence. Whilst finance has for some years remained within the confines of statute, the procedures have been updated. Court structures have also changed. Keeping track of such frequent changes is a monumental task.

Writing a handbook with such a moving target carries considerable risk. By the time the draft arrives at the printing stage, proposed changes in law and procedure may have come into force. The Ministry of Justice or the President of the Family Division could have presented recommendations or a consultation document threatening to jeopardise some or even all that has gone before.

I have practised in most areas of Family Law: handbooks have been available to me, but most have focused on individual subjects. Few have provided me with a global view of the many areas making up the subject of Family Law. More importantly, none has given me much detailed guidance on how things happen in practice.

This handbook is intended therefore to be intensely practical.

I begin the book with the law firm: where the practitioner works: who works there and what they do. I then move on to the most important people, our clients, and how that professional relationship develops over time. I explore how we can best help our clients both outside and inside the court room. I look at a full range of orders and procedures.

I hope this book is useful to all those who have chosen to practise in an area of law which at times is sensitive and heart breaking, yet so rewarding and valuable for those who benefit from it.

PART A

FIRMS, FILES & CLIENTS

CHAPTER 1

THE STRUCTURE OF LAW FIRMS

A law firm is a business entity formed by one or more lawyers to engage in the practice of law. The primary purpose of a law firm is to advise clients (individuals or corporations) about their legal rights and responsibilities, and to represent clients in family, civil or criminal cases, business transactions, and other matters in which legal advice and other assistance are sought.

Law firms are organised in a variety of ways, depending on the work which the firm undertakes. Common arrangements include:

A sole proprietorship (also known as a sole trader) is a law firm owned and run by one person in which there is no legal distinction between the owner and the business itself. A sole trader does not necessarily work alone and may employ other people.

The sole trader receives all profits and has full responsibility for all losses and debts of the business. Every asset of the business is owned by the proprietor, and all debts of the business are that of the proprietor personally. Sole proprietors may use a business name other than their legal name.

In contrast to the sole proprietor is a partnership, which has at least two owners. A partnership is an association of persons has the following major features:

- Must be created by agreement

- Formed by two or more persons

- The owners are jointly and severally responsible for any legal actions and debts the firm may face, unless otherwise provided by law or in the agreement.

- It is a partnership in which partners share equally in both responsibility and liability.

- Subject to contrary agreement, the assets of the business are owned on behalf of all partners, and they are each personally liable, jointly and severally, for business debts and taxes

The *Limited Liability Partnerships Act 2000* confers separate personality on limited liability partnerships. A limited liability partnership (LLP) is a partnership in which some or all partners have limited liabilities. In an LLP, each partner is not responsible or liable for another partner's misconduct or negligence. In an LLP, some or all partners have a form of limited liability similar to that of the shareholders of a corporation.

Law firms are typically organised around partners, who are joint owners and business directors of the legal operation; associates, who are employees of the firm with the prospect of becoming partners; and a variety of staff employees, providing paralegal, clerical, and other support services.

Size

Law firms vary widely in size. The smallest law firms are lawyers practicing alone, who form the vast majority of lawyers in England and Wales. Smaller firms tend to focus on particular specialties of the law (eg, family, criminal defence, personal injury, conveyancing); larger firms may be composed of several specialised practice groups, allowing the firm to offer a variety of services to their clients. The largest law firms have more than 1,000 lawyers. These firms are sometimes called 'mega firm' often have offices on several countries.

Boutique Law firms

Lawyers in small cities and towns may still have traditional general practices, but some lawyers are highly specialised due to the overwhelming complexity of the law today. Thus, some small firms in the cities specialise in practicing only one kind of law (for example family law) and are sometimes called boutique law firms

Virtual Law Firms

A recent development has been the appearance of the virtual law firm, a firm with a virtual business address but no brick & mortar office location open to the public, using modern telecommunications to operate from remote locations. It provides legal services to clients, avoiding the costs of maintaining a physical premises with lower overheads than traditional law firms. This lower cost structure allows virtual law firms to bill clients at a lower level.

Location

Most law firms are located in office buildings of various sizes, ranging from modest one-story buildings to high rise blocks. Some are located in high streets of small towns and others in commercial centres of large cities.

CHAPTER 2

INTERNAL WORKINGS OF A LAW FIRM

Whilst there is some variation from firm to firm, most of them usually operate in a similar way.

Most UK law firms are arranged in a pyramid structure, although there can be some variety, so the explanation below of how they work should only be taken as a loose guide. You may see solicitors referred to as 'fee-earners' – which is any member of staff whose work directly generates income for the firm. Listed below are the types of "fee-earner".

Partners

Partners usually sit at the very top of the pyramid. Most law firms operate as partnerships, which are co-owned by partners. There will usually be a Senior or Managing Partner (sometimes both). In some law firms, all partners have equal stake in the business and have an equal say in how the business operates. In other law firms, there will be an internal hierarchy within the Partners themselves depending on the amount of equity they hold, or whether they are salaried. All cases / matters handled by a law firm will be done under the supervision of a Partner.

Legal Directors

Legal Directors usually sit just below Partners. Not all law firms have this role. A Legal Director typically oversees a lot of business operations at the firm, will run their own cases, and carry a lot of senior managerial responsibility. They generally oversee one particular area of business operations that they specialise in. Many law firms appoint Legal Directors as a stepping-stone to them being made a partner.

Senior Associates and Associates

An Associate is usually another term for a qualified and practicing Solicitor. You'll sometimes see Senior Associates titled or something similar. An Associate with more than 5 years PQE is regarded as fairly senior in a law firm, and will sometimes take on additional responsibilities as a Senior Associate.

Law Firm Trainees

A Trainee is someone who has completed their formal legal education and who has a Training Contract with a law firm. This means they will complete approximately two years paid training with the firm before qualifying as a Solicitor. A Trainee will sometimes complete work suitable for more experienced paralegals, and sometimes complete work suitable for lawyers. Training Contract placements are very limited and highly sought after. Some law firms are currently in the process of phasing out traditional Training Contracts, in favour of the new Solicitor's Qualifying Examination (SQE).

Paralegals

A Paralegal is, essentially, a legal professional who is not yet qualified. Some paralegals will be fee earners, depending on the nature of the tasks they are performing. Paralegals perform an enormous range of legal tasks based around routine legal matters. This includes reviewing documents and drafting contracts, to preparing bundles and filing court documents. A good law firm will choose good paralegals and invest in their success, and paralegals will often become a key part of running a case.

Non-fee earners

Not every employee of a law firm is a fee-earner. There are a range of law firm employees whose time is not billed to clients. This could include accountants, human resource staff, administrative workers, marketing executives, or anyone else working non-billable time. Law firms often operate a system of paralegals, associates and partners, all working to meet the demands of the client. Workloads are often challenging, so each member of staff of the organisation plays an important role in assisting and supporting the fee earners in achieving their goal.

Law firms and profitability

In simple terms, law firms make money by hiring out their fee earners to clients and charging for their time. These are all legal professionals employed by the business who can work for clients for a fee, such as paralegals or associates. When law firms are hired by their clients, they agree the work that needs to be done. This referred to as a 'matter' or 'case'. To make a profit, a law firm simply needs to generate more client fees by hiring out its fee earners to work on client matters than it expends in operational costs.

Billable hours

Law firms traditionally make money by charging their fee earners to client matters on an hourly basis. This is based on billable hours of work.

The billable hour is, simply put, an hour's labour that a fee earner has spent working on a client matter. Each billable hour is based on units of time that are recorded by fee earners.

Units of time are quite an archaic unit of measurement. Each unit of time is 6 minutes of work. This might seem a little odd, but dividing each billable hour into ten 6 minute increments helps law firms and their clients track billable time more easily. When law firms and their clients agree that 10 units of time make up a billable hour, each hour worked by a fee earner can then be billed to the client, and the law firm can turn a profit.

Recording billable hours

Law firms use software to keep track how many units of time their fee earners have worked on client matters. If you're a fee-earner working for a client, you will be expected to record the time you have spent on each matter. This is done by recording your units of time alongside a narrative. A narrative is a short summary of how you spent that time. These narratives are often sent directly to the client in order to justify how much they are being charged by the law firm, so keeping them accurate is very important. Anything written in narratives could be checked by a client so they need to be carefully worded.

Measuring productivity

Law firms like to track productivity and how much of the fee earner's time is spent on chargeable matters. Each fee earner will be expected to perform above a fixed target. This to ensure they are using their time efficiently. Annual targets that are frequently measured monthly or even weekly.

CHAPTER 3

ROLES IN A LAW FIRM

Law costs draftsman

Law costs draftsmen ensure that a firm's clients are properly charged for work undertaken on the clients' behalf. They also help apportion costs between the two sets of legal advisers at the end of long and complex cases. In some instances, they represent clients in court when there is an issue over costs.

Visit the Association of Costs Lawyers website:
https://www.associationofcostslawyers.co.uk

Legal cashier

Legal cashiers usually work in solicitors' practices. They keep financial records and keep solicitors informed of the financial position of the firm.

Legal executive

A chartered legal executive can work in a legal office and has the option to later qualify as a solicitor through further vocational training. Fully qualified chartered legal executive lawyers will have their own clients and represent them in court, where appropriate. The main difference between solicitors and legal executives is that the training of legal executives is narrower. Legal executives have often studied to the same level as a solicitor, but they have specialised in a particular area of law and completed fewer subjects overall.

Visit the CILEx website:
https://www.cilex.org.uk

Legal secretary

Legal secretaries provide secretarial and clerical support to solicitors, barristers and the law courts. They deal with large quantities of correspondence and help prepare documents such as wills, divorce petitions and witness statements. Legal secretaries are specialists because legal documents are composed differently from other commercial documents.

Visit the Institute of Legal Secretaries and PAs website:
https://www.institutelegalsecretaries.com

Notary

Notaries are qualified lawyers appointed by the Archbishop of Canterbury and regulated by the Master of the Faculties. Notaries practice under rules very similar to those of solicitors', including renewing a practicing certificate, keeping client money separate and maintaining insurance. Notaries authenticate and certify signatures and documents, and often also practice as solicitors.

Visit the Notaries Society website:
https://www.thenotariessociety.org.uk

Paralegal

Paralegals assist lawyers in their work. They undertake some of the same work as lawyers but do not usually give advice to clients. The paralegal is a relatively modern phenomenon in British legal circles. The role has transferred across from the US where paralegals have operated in a support role in law firms for many years.

The duties of a paralegal will vary according to the type of firm and practice area that is worked in. Generic paralegal tasks may include research and drafting documents, attending client meetings and document management. They might prepare reports to help lawyers prepare their case.

Solicitor

Solicitors work in many different areas of law and offer many different services. Solicitors are confidential advisers and will often have direct contact with their clients, providing expert legal advice and assistance in a range of situations.

Everyday issues solicitors deal with include:

- dealing with relationship breakdown

- protecting the rights of individuals by advising people of their rights, ensuring they are treated fairly by public or private bodies

- supporting the community by undertaking legal aid work or spending a portion of their time providing free help for those unable to pay for legal services

- representing clients personally in the lower courts (Magistrates' courts, County Court and tribunals) and with specialist training are also able to represent them in higher courts (Crown Court, High Court, Court of Appeal and the Supreme Court)

The Law Society of England and Wales represents, promotes and supports solicitors in England and Wales:
https://www.lawsociety.org.uk/en

Arbitrator and mediator

Arbitration and mediation are non-judicial and alternative ways to resolve disputes, without going to court. Arbitrators and mediators are neutral, which means they will not take sides and cannot provide advice.

They are often experts in the field of what the dispute is about, and will reach a decision after hearing from both sides of the dispute.

Visit the Chartered Institute of Arbitrators website: https://www.ciarb.org/home

CHAPTER 4

INFORMATION AHEAD OF THE FIRST MEETING

Prior to the first meeting with your client, you should ascertain, often by telephone or email, the following:

- **The client's financial resources**

Check whether the client is eligible for legal aid. If the client is eligible for legal aid and it is not offered by your firm, you have an obligation to inform them that such assistance may be provided by another firm.

- **Details to carry out a conflict check**

It is worth checking whether the other party has been known by any other names, such as a maiden name or previous married names, in order to be thorough in the conflict check. If there is a conflict, you should be prepared to recommend another Solicitor to the client.

- **Charging**

It is important at this stage to set out the charging structure, whether the initial meeting is chargeable and if so, on what basis. Clarity at the outset will start the relationship on the appropriate footing. It is also a regulatory condition.

- **Identification**

When arranging an appointment, it should be explained to the client the initial information/documentation required in order to comply with the Money Laundering Regulations. The client can bring these to the initial appointment. This will avoid delay in accepting instructions. A valid passport or driving licence and evidence of their current address should normally be presented at the first meeting.

- **Telephone advice**

It may be that urgent advice is required by telephone in order to protect the client's interim position. You should be cautious when providing such advice without full details from the client. If there are facts that could change the position, this should be made clear.

CHAPTER 5

THE FIRST MEETING WITH THE CLIENT

The first meeting with a client to take instructions on a family law matter is foundational. It is likely to establish the Solicitor and client relationship for months and even years to come. For this reason careful thought needs to be given as to how the meeting is conducted, what is said and agreed and how the work is to be funded.

Each initial interview has **four main goals**:

1. To get to know the client.

2. To obtain important information.

3. To reduce anxiety

4. To clarify the clients' expectations.

The first direct contact with your client will usually take place in a face-to-face meeting. Steps should be taken to ensure that the meeting is allocated to an appropriate Solicitor within the firm who can advise the client correctly. Ensure that the relationship with the client remains professional and inspires a high degree of confidence in the service given. The initial meeting will be an opportunity to obtain all the necessary and most relevant background information. It is important to remember that clients will not always know what is relevant and it is therefore important to ask probing questions and to elicit as much detail as possible.

You should maintain an objective approach whilst offering understanding, practical advice and support. Remember, however, that the client is there for legal assistance. You are not there to be a personal friend offering support or counselling. If the client does stray into areas that it would be more appropriate to be dealt with via counsellors, family therapists, parenting courses etc, you may be able to recommend such services and signpost them to agencies that can help.

- **Ensure the interview is in private and take steps to avoid interruptions**

Any meeting should be in a place where the discussions with your client will not be overheard. This will reassure the client as well as underlining confidentiality. An interview room specially allocated for this purpose is commonly used in many law firms. Avoid taking telephone calls and having interruptions. Turn off your mobile telephone.

- **Allow sufficient time to cover matters adequately**

The client must never feel the meeting is being rushed whilst discussing personal matters with you. Avoid a clash or overlap of appointments.

- **Identity checks and money laundering**

You can conduct an initial interview before verifying the client's identity if you are only providing legal advice, and not doing transactional work. If you take on the client's case you should verify their identity in line with the anti-money laundering regulations.

- **Use of Pro forma**

A client instruction sheet is a means of capturing all relevant client information. This includes: contact details, information about any children, partner's details, accommodation, financial circumstances and the information required for example, a divorce petition. This may be completed in the meeting with the client or sent to the client in advance of a meeting.

- Give advice

Once you have taken the necessary information, you should advise the client accordingly. Sometimes your advice goes beyond what the client expects but this is necessary to provide the complete picture of the issues involved.

- Make a full attendance note

If possible, a full attendance note should be completed during the meeting itself either in outline or with full details. If this is not possible ensure that the attendance note is completed in full immediately after the meeting. It is common for solicitors to send a copy of this attendance note to the client following the meeting either attached to the client care letter or as a separate document. The client can be asked to confirm that the contents of the attendance note is agreed. This will avoid future misunderstandings as to the content and nature of the original discussions.

- Confidentiality

You should make it clear that you will deal with all matters in a confidential manner and that information regarding the case will not be disclosed to third parties without the client's permission.

It can be difficult to address potential inconsistencies in a client's account of facts at a first meeting when the lawyer/client relationship has not had the chance to develop. If there are any concerns, explain the duty of confidentiality owed to the client and the importance of being open and honest when providing instructions. Explain also the likely consequences of providing false and misleading information and that you have a duty not to mislead the court on any information provided.

Whilst confidentiality is being discussed, it is important to explain the exceptions. Where there are concerns regarding money laundering, or if there is a risk of significant physical or mental harm to a child and/or others, you should explain your duty not to withhold relevant information or to mislead the court either by actions or omissions.

If a client is unwilling to disclose information, you must emphasise the likelihood of any non-disclosure being discovered in due course, the risk of adverse inference and costs orders as a result.

- **Explore the possibility of a reconciliation**

Separating parties may wish to find out where they stand. Commencing proceedings or taking any steps may not be appropriate if they are not yet certain that the relationship is over. You should provide advice and referrals to any appropriate services if this is the case. As a Mediation Information & Assessment Meeting (MIAM) is obligatory in some cases, it has become common to discuss the various alternative methods of resolving family disputes. Depending on the circumstances an offer of direct discussion, mediation, collaborative law and arbitration can be an advantage for clients and should be discussed at the outset to inform of the full range of options available. Further details these options are found later in this handbook.

- **Explain the approach you will take**

It is worthwhile to explain early on that, whilst a robust approach may be adopted, you will comply with the Law Society, Chartered Institute of Legal Executives and Resolution Codes of Practice and that you will not conduct the litigation in any unduly confrontational way. Explain the benefits of working in this way. If the client has unrealistic expectations of what the proceedings may achieve, inform them as early as possible as to what may be a realistic outcome of the legal process. This can be linked with the discussion of alternative dispute resolution procedures which offer greater flexibility in finding tailored solutions.

- **Explain your role**

Many new clients will not have used a solicitor before so they won't be familiar with the process. You should explain your role and the services you provide, as well as those you do not provide. You should also discuss your responsibilities and those of your client. Confirm these details in writing, the name and status of the person dealing with the case and the person with overall responsibility.

- **Timescales**

Discuss the timescales for completing any work. It is often difficult to give accurate times and dates when events will take place so you should be cautious about giving precise information. If you do so, you should make it clear that many matters within court proceedings are outside your professional control and that you cannot be bound to such information.

- **Advice or support services from third parties**

Consider whether it is worthwhile for the client to seek further advice on specific points at this stage for example, on tax or financial planning issues. If so, try to make a recommendation based on the client's needs and personality. Consider providing any documentation straightaway to enable progress. In financial matters, consider providing a blank Form E so the client can start collating the relevant information and decide whether third party advice is needed such as information as the value of the matrimonial home or the current value of a pension fund.

- **Provide details of your future costs**

It is often difficult to provide an accurate estimate of costs at the outset of a case, but it is essential that the client can make an informed decision regarding the risks of litigation and other options available. It is also important to explain the potential risks of a costs award being made against a party within proceedings.

Under the Solicitors Regulation Authority (SRA) Standards and Regulations, you must give your client the best information possible about the likely overall cost of a matter at the start, and as their matter progresses. These may include:

- agreeing a fixed fee
- giving a realistic estimate of the overall cost
- giving a forecast within a possible range, or
- explaining why costs cannot be fixed or realistically estimated

You must explain how charges are calculated, and you should provide information at the first interview on:

- hourly rates and an estimate of the time to be charged
- whether rates are likely to increase
- expected disbursements and when they will be due
- potential liability for others' costs
- VAT

This information must be confirmed in writing following the first meeting and before any work is undertaken on behalf of the client.

- **Consider Unbundling**

Law firms are becoming increasingly flexible in terms of the services they provide. If a client does not want a solicitor to conduct the entire case on their behalf, it can sometimes be possible to have an "unbundled" service. This means that the solicitor acts for the client in certain parts of the case and the client deals with other parts as a Litigant in Person, although the solicitor is available to give advice if needed. This can be a much more cost-effective way of dealing with a matter. You may wish to discuss this option with your client at the initial meeting.

- **Take copies of all relevant documents**

The client may hand you documents you have requested to comply with the money laundering regulations. It is important that you take copies for your file returning the originals to your client for safe keeping. There may also be other documents which you need to see and take copies of, for example, divorce papers or a court application. It is good practice to take copies for your file and return the original documents to the client. This will ensure that your client has all the information in their possession for future reference.

- **Give the client appropriate leaflets**

This can cover the subjects discussed but also other information to assist the client. Some lawyers often prepare booklets and brochures that are handed to family law clients at the first meeting.

CHAPTER 6

FOLLOW UP WORK AFTER THE FIRST MEETING

- **Client Care letter**

All firms have an obligation to provide information about their services at the point of engagement with a client and as a matter progresses. When they begin working with a client, firms often provide this information in a client care letter. There are some definitive information requirements:

- Information about your regulatory status and how that affects the protections available to the client

- Costs information, including the likely overall cost of the matter

- Instructions about how to complain

- An explanation of your duties to the court

- Where relevant, information about referrals, introductions, fee sharing and any separate businesses that might have a commercial interest in the client's matter.

- **Agree a 'to do' list with your client**

This will ensure that you and your client know what is expected of each other. Your client may need to provide you with documents or information before taking matters forward. If on the other hand, the client does not wish to take things further, or would prefer to take time to reflect on the advice received, you should be understanding and agree the best way to make contact in future, if the client decides to do so.

- **Funding and money on account**

Your client care letter will set out the basis on which your client will be charged for your services. Many firms will request a payment on account of costs and expenses before any further work is undertaken. This request is often made immediately after the initial meeting with the client.

- **Make contact with opponents or others**

If your client's opponent has instructed solicitors and you are aware of their identity, you should make contact with them soon after the initial meeting with your client informing them of your interest. This can be by telephone, email or letter. This ensures that your client will not receive any correspondence or communication direct from the firm concerned. If your client is facing pending court proceedings you would usually make contact with the court and the other parties informing them of your interest. If you are instructed to represent your client in those proceedings, you should file a Notice of Acting with the court and serve a copy on the opposing party.

- **File papers with court or other agencies**

If instructed to do so, you will take all necessary steps to act for your client including the drafting and filing of all appropriate documents.

CHAPTER 7

VULNERABLE CLIENTS – MATTERS TO LOOK OUT FOR

It could be said that all family law clients should be considered as vulnerable in some measure. They are usually in a state of heightened emotion when they first meet with their Solicitor, who is asking them to explain very personal and upsetting matters with someone they have not met before. There are, of course, very different degrees of vulnerability and how best to support and assist our client is not easy. The following sets out some guidance on working with vulnerable clients.

Who is a vulnerable client?

This list is focused on those who would be seen to be more vulnerable than most and where more than your usual good client care might be needed:

- children

- alcohol or substance misusers

- those with a physical disability or illness

- those with a mental illness

- the elderly

- those who do not speak English as their first language;

- those with a learning difficulty.

- victims of domestic abuse

It may not be apparent at your first meeting that your client has any difficulty giving you instructions, but you have a duty to keep this under review.

- **Children**

Children will always be considered vulnerable clients or witnesses in any family law case. Should they be a party to proceedings they will usually be represented by a member of the Law Society's Children Panel. The members of that panel will have been assessed as qualified to represent children either through a children's guardian or directly. You should not normally accept instructions from a child client unless you are a member of that Panel.

- **Mental Health/Lack of Capacity**

One of the most difficult areas for practitioners is raising the issue of a client's mental health or a concern regarding their capacity to provide you with instructions. It is a highly sensitive issue, and many sufferers of mental ill health or someone who has learning difficulties may have little or no insight into their own difficulties. If you are concerned that your client should be a protected party you will need to carefully consider the guidance in **Part 15 of the FPR with PDs 15A and 15B and the Mental Capacity Act 2005 (MCA 2005).**

- **Disability**

Your client may have no issue regarding their capacity to provide instructions to you. However, a physical incapacity or disability may be something that requires careful consideration so the client is fully able to participate. Your office should be accessible for your client or you will need to consider an alternative venue. Liaise with the person responsible for ensuring equality and diversity in your place of work.

The **Solicitors Regulation Authority (SRA) Code of Conduct Handbook** makes it clear in **Chapter 2** that:

> ... *you make reasonable adjustments to ensure that disabled clients, employees or managers are not placed at a substantial disadvantage compared to those who are not disabled, and you do not pass on the costs of these adjustments to these disabled clients, employees or managers.*

- **Alcohol/Drug misuse**

It would be inappropriate to take instructions from a client who is under the influence of alcohol or drugs. If you are concerned that this might be the case, you need to raise this sensitively with the client. If they confirm that they are under the influence or you remain concerned that that is the case even though they have denied it and not provided any other explanation for that behaviour, you must advise them that you will not be able to take instructions at that meeting. You will need to carefully explain why it would not be appropriate for you to take instructions in those circumstances and to arrange a further appointment, making it clear that they must not drink/use drugs before the meeting. This should be followed up with a letter setting out the advice as a record for your file.

- **Clients with a Learning Difficulty**

A client with a learning difficulty is more likely to feel intimidated by legal terminology and you will need to find ways to simplify complex matters for them to be able to understand and engage in proceedings. Clients with learning difficulties are often heavily reliant on family, friends or carers to assist them in their day-to-day lives. If your client attends your offices with a supporter, be careful to listen and direct your conversation to the client rather than their supporter, and allow extra time to accommodate their communication needs. Take the time to check the client has understood the key points of your advice and as with any client, adapt your practice to meet their needs.

You may meet a new client who has difficulty with reading and writing. It is important that you are aware of your client's literacy ability at the earliest opportunity. You may need to adjust your normal practice in respect of communicating with your clients. It is best to ask your client directly and sensitively about their reading ability. You could also ask the client to read something to you in your meeting, perhaps a Form of Authority or another document you are asking them to sign. If your client is unable to read you should find out if they would like you to telephone to read letters to them or have a trusted friend or family member who can read important documents to them. There will of course need to be consideration in relation to the confidential nature of court documents. **Rule 12.75 of the FPR** covers this:

> A party or the legal representative of a party, on behalf of and upon the instructions of that party, may communicate information relating to the proceedings to any person where necessary to enable that party […] by confidential discussion, to obtain support, advice or assistance in the conduct of the proceedings.

> You will need to ensure that the recipient of the information is aware that they must not disclose the contents to anyone, and it is best practice to get them to sign a declaration confirming their understanding of the confidential nature of the information they will read whilst supporting your client.

- **Those who do not speak English as their first language**

You will need to ascertain as soon as possible whether a client does not speak English as their first language and whether they will need the assistance of an interpreter. If it becomes apparent that your client needs help, it is good practice to rearrange your meeting to ensure they have proper support in place. You should remember that while they may be able to speak English to a good level, their understanding of your advice may not be so good, particularly the legal language. You will also need to understand from them their reading ability and whether your written communication will need to be translated. It may be that external support from an interpreter is needed for meetings, telephone conferences and hearings.

- **The Elderly**

An elderly client is at a higher risk of physical and/or mental impairment and this will need to be considered when advising clients who are elderly.

- **Victims of Domestic Abuse**

The definition of domestic abuse as provided by the (then) President of the Family Division, Sir James Munby in **Practice Direction 12J** of the **FPR 2010** is:

> ... *any incident or pattern of incidents of controlling, coercive or threatening behaviour, violence or abuse between those aged 16 or over who are, or have been, intimate partners or family members regardless of gender or sexuality. This can encompass, but is not limited to psychological, physical, sexual, financial, or emotional abuse. Domestic abuse also includes culturally specific forms of abuse including, but not limited to, forced marriage honour-based violence, dowry-related abuse and transnational marriage abandonment."*

Identifying and assessing risk

Your client may have no hesitation in informing you of the domestic abuse they have suffered, and you will be able to ask them openly about this in order to establish how you can best advise them. Other clients will not be so forthcoming about abuse and may actively avoid disclosing this information to you. If your client has not sought support and assistance from an outside agency in relation to the domestic abuse they have suffered, then you should signpost them to local services who can assist them.

Further resources

- Law Society's *Practice Note on Meeting the needs of vulnerable clients*.

- The Solicitors Regulation Authority (SRA) has released a document *'Providing services to people who are vulnerable'* available as a PDF from the SRA website.

- Resolution has provided a domestic abuse alert toolkit, which should be used in all first appointments with clients, and see also the good practice guidance on domestic abuse.

CHAPTER 8

MANAGING CLIENTS' EXPECTATIONS

For some clients, the single most important thing on their mind is their file. Some clients expect their work to be completed immediately. You may have to take measures to protect your own professional position.

Some basic principles

a. Even the most outstanding service will never be enough if your client's expectations are unrealistic. This realisation is an important place to start. The client is the one who may unknowingly hold expectations that are unrealistic, impractical and sometimes impossible. However, you are responsible for tactfully recalibrating those expectations to a level that can be met. Getting a clear picture of your client's preconceived ideas and expectations is vital. You should not wait until you have failed to meet an expectation to try to overturn it. Instead, ask your client at your first meeting:

- What action do they want you to take?

- What is their budget?

- What are their main concerns?

- What are their deadlines?

This will give you a good starting place to understand their needs and help a client have an understanding of unrealistic expectations.

b. The beginning of a matter is a good time to establish the preferred method of communication, response times for email enquiries, your availability to take phone calls and how often you will issue progressive invoices.

c. A major source of anxiety for the client is the unknown. Provide genuine reassurance and take the time to make sure they thoroughly understand the legal issues and what is involved.

d. Be clear on an agreed financial budget.

e. Gently reshape expectations where necessary. This may include providing frank and candid advice as to the legal realities of their situation and whether or not the anticipated outcomes can be achieved.

f. Successful client management requires continual work. Be proactive with communication and diarise a regular brief update. The failure to keep the client informed is the most common reason for complaint. Telephone, emails and text messages assist in this. You can, after all, charge for the calls and other forms of communications you make.

g. Maintain your professional standards.

h. Don't mislead or exaggerate to a client about anything. Honesty may be painful, but it is the best policy.

i. Don't promise what you can't deliver.

j. Don't become emotionally involved in their case. Maintain your professional detachment.

k. Be up front (and confirm in writing) about fees and costs.

l. Define your role. Work in partnership with your client – joint ownership/joint responsibility. Decide with your client what actions are required. Give your client work to do. Remind them that whatever they can do to help saves you time and saves them money.

m. Unless otherwise agreed with the client, copy the client in on everything important that comes in or goes out on their case.

n. Always return client calls.

o. Document everything. Keep copies. Keep a record of what is agreed. Adopt the principal: 'If it didn't happen in writing it didn't happen'.

p. If you don't know, don't bluff it.

q. Think carefully about the special needs for different clients: aggressive or difficult clients, those mentally ill, those illiterate, those with learning difficulty, those with language difficulties.

r. If your client won't follow your advice ask them to sign a document which states that they have been advised and have declined to accept this advice.

s. When necessary, debrief with your team members.

t. Check files for key dates, monitor costs, keep within costs estimate and ensure that records and communication is up to date.

Complaints

Complaints will arise from time to time. There is a professional obligation for you to:

- Ensure that you cooperate in attempting to resolve a complaint

- Ensure that you participate in a procedure for handling complaints in relation to the legal services you provide

- Ensure that a client is informed in writing at the time of engagement about:

    o their right to complain to you about your services and your charges

    o how a complaint can be made and to whom

    o any right they have to make a complaint to the *Legal Ombudsman* and when they can make any such complaint.

- Ensure that when clients have made a complaint to you, if this has not been resolved to the client's satisfaction within 8 weeks following the making of a complaint they are informed in writing:

    o of any right they have to complain to the *Legal Ombudsman*, the time frame for doing so and full details of how to contact the *Legal Ombudsman*

    o if a complaint has been brought and your complaints procedure has been exhausted

    o that you cannot settle the complaint

    o of the name and website address of an alternative dispute resolution (ADR) approved body which would be competent to deal with the complaint.

Solicitors and their employees must follow the Solicitors Regulation Authority (SRA) Code of Conduct.

CHAPTER 9

MANAGEMENT OF A FAMILY LAW FILE

We need to remind ourselves that we are part of a business so it is important that we should be as efficient as possible, providing the best service for our client, as well as making the maximum profit for those who own the business. This is reflected in the way the client file is handled.

The Golden Rule – Good File Management

Keeping documents organised and accessible can make a huge difference to your law firm's success. When you have a good legal filing system, you can find and access legal files more easily. This makes you more productive, efficient, and effective as a Solicitor. Your files should be logically organised and you should be able to quickly search and find legal documents. You also need to develop a filing system that will not become obsolete a year later. The same file management principles apply to the electronic files stored on your computer.

- Files should be kept in good order and be easy to follow enabling another colleague to quickly assimilate what the case is about should you be absent from the office. It is helpful to have a file management structure within a firm so that, if the Solicitor with conduct is unavailable, another member of staff can assist a client with queries.

- It will ensure key dates are diarised, regular file reviews and meetings with the rest of your team to discuss cases to ensure that even inactive files are dealt with at a pace that suits the client. This will also help towards risk management processes too and help to avoid complaints.

- Access to legal case management software takes care of the time-consuming administrative tasks and document production, allowing you to provide the highest quality of personal service to your clients. These are often designed for all family law procedures, including matrimonial, ancillary relief, Children's Act claims and injunction proceedings.

- File Management is a real issue. It is not just a question of having a tidy file. It should have an order to it. A fee earner may know where to find things in the file but others should too. Many firms will have a system that runs through the whole of the family department which is an ideal policy. A well-kept file saves time, energy and unnecessary frustrations.

- **Client care letter**

This is a professional requirement as well as a good practice to adopt. A well drafted client care letter will create a good foundation for the client/solicitor relationship. It is essentially a contract between your firm and the client. The client will know from that letter: the advice you have given, an idea of costs in terms of fees, and an estimate as to how long the case will take to complete. It will be a useful reference point for both sides. A badly drawn client care letter will be the very opposite and is likely to lead to problems. Extra time spent on making sure the terms of engagement are set out well and clear will pay dividends in the long term.

https://www.sra.org.uk/solicitors/guidance/client-care-letters/

- **Files opened for each client**

Your firm will almost certainly have their own way of opening and keeping a client file. It has become usual for each client of the firm to have their own unique number. Each time a file is opened for a particular client, the same number will be used followed by a decimal point for each matter.

- **Sections of files**

A client file will be divided up into sections: correspondence, emails, pleadings, court orders, witness statements, experts reports. These are common examples. This makes it much easier to locate a document. Clear labelling is vital. Computer case management systems are geared up for this purpose.

- **Safeguard confidentiality**

Files held by law firms are kept in the strictest confidence. Clients need to be assured that the information held in their file will not be communicated to anyone outside your firm unless permission has been given.

https://www.sra.org.uk/solicitors/guidance/confidentiality-client-information/

- **File access and checks**

Your client file should be kept in a form that allows not only you but others in the firm to gain access to client information easily and efficiently. If you are not in the office it is vital that others are able to look at the file and gain whatever details they need quickly. It's worth remembering that the file is kept by the firm and not only the fee earner. It will also allow the firm to undertake regular file checks to ensure the case is moving forward to plan and that important work and time limits are not missed.

- **Billing and costs update**

As your firm is a business it follows that clients will need to be billed for work done on a regular basis. Your firm may have a procedure for billing clients. The client may be sent an invoice each month or whatever period of time the firm has agreed. This ensures financial stability and requires fee earners carry a degree of responsibility in ensuring that the work is done, billed and paid for.

https://www.lawsociety.org.uk/en/public/for-public-visitors/using-a-solicitor/paying-for-a-solicitor

- **Time recording**

A fee earner will know how much to bill a client by keeping a record of how much time is spent working on a particular file. Computer systems make this task relatively easy. Disciplined time recording enables the firm and client to know how much is owed at any one time. This is a sign of an efficient and well-tuned business.

- **Attendance notes**

Keeping a record of what happens in a case is vital. It could be an attendance on a client, a court hearing, telephone call or other conversation. It is impossible to remember what has happened and what is said on every file. For this reason it is important that a fee earner keeps a written record in the form of an attendance note for future reference. It should be in a form that is accurate and sufficiently detailed to cover all the points in the conversation and time taken. It can also be a time record for any future billing.

- **Keeping a diary**

Family cases frequently involve court hearings and time limits as well as meetings of various kinds. Keeping a diary is an important part of an efficient work pattern. It should avoid a clash of dates and missed appointments and court hearings. Many family departments keep a unified diary for all their fee earners. This makes it possible to keep track of the commitments of each fee earner in the department. Some fee earners also keep their own individual diary.

- **Correspondence with opponents (and others)**

Communication with other solicitors is part of the work of a family Solicitor. This can be in the form of letters and emails. A separate section of the client file is often set aside for this purpose. This enables the fee earner to refer easily to these communications without having to trawl though the whole file to locate the communication in question.

- **Keep clients informed**

A major cause of complaint from clients in running a family file is that the client is not kept in touch with developments. Keeping clients informed is not difficult. Emails and text messages are quick and easy. Telephone calls and letters can take a little longer. Most clients don't expect a detailed update but a brief report is enough for them to know they are not forgotten and to be reassured you are on their case. Goodwill can be engendered by a brief telephone call or email to keep the client in touch.

If a fee earner undertakes work for a client, email or telephone the client to inform them of this. If your client knows you have completed the work he/she will have the more confidence in you and your efficiency. You are, after all, paid to do this work.

- **Clients should approve important letters and proposals**

A fee earner needs to communicate well on a client's behalf. Instructions may have been received from a client to put forward an offer of settlement or other proposals. It is good practice to send a written copy of the proposals to the client before being dispatched to the opponent. This will ensure that the client is happy with the details. Doing this by email is often most efficient but a letter is another option.

Ask the client to confirm that the proposals reflect the instructions you have received. Once the client has given approval, the proposals can be sent and a copy sent to the client.

If this does not happen, the fee earner may later find the client has had a change of mind or the communication does not quite fit with the original instructions. Misunderstandings of this kind between the fee earner and a client can lead to difficulties, including complaints.

- **Send copies of documents to client**

Remember that the file you hold is owned by your client. They are entitled to know about everything that happens in the case. You must never hold back information that the client is entitled to know about. This includes documents that come in and go out. It is good practice to send copies of all relevant documents to the client. There may be exceptions such as unpleasant or abusive correspondence which could lead to your client being upset or distressed. In this case, you may need to think of communicating the information in an appropriate form. Never be in a situation where a client says 'You never told me that'.

- **Returning telephone calls and replies to emails to client**

Devise a policy for returning ALL telephone calls and emails. This is the right thing to do. It falls under the same heading as keeping the client informed. A failure to do this can give the impression of being inefficient and not caring. Remember, you will be paid for doing so.

- **Persistent telephone callers**

This is not an easy subject to deal with. There is no blueprint. You need to check that you are playing your part in keeping the client informed. If you have done what you can and the client is calling regularly for no good reason, then sending a bill to the client on a regular basis can do the trick. If your client is behaving unreasonably there may need to be a discussion as to whether the lawyer/client relationship should continue.

- **Unbundling**

This is a subject that has become more common in the running of a family file. Your firm may have some experience of this and indeed have clients who have agreed to instruct your firm on this basis. Traditionally, a law firm will act for a client in all family law matters, for example, divorce, children, money and so on. In the case of unbundling, the client may choose to deal with divorce and children matters personally but ask you to deal with financial matters only. You need to be clear who is doing what and that there is no misunderstanding on this. You client care letter should be carefully drawn up to reflect the correct position. Usually, the client is keen to ensure that legal costs are kept to a minimum or that a fixed fee is agreed. The relationship between solicitor and client is very different from a full retainer relationship. Both parties need to proceed with caution and a clear understanding from the outset is key to providing and receiving an unbundled legal service.

https://www.sra.org.uk/sra/news/sra-update-97-unbundling/

http://https//resolution.org.uk/resolutions-good-practice-guides/good-practice-guide-for-family-lawyers-working-with-clients/

- **Legal Aid and amendments**

For those who work in a firm where legal aid is undertaken, fee earners will know that all legal costs in a file are covered by the legal aid certificate issued by the Legal Aid Agency. The certificate sets out the nature of the case, what is covered and any limits or conditions attached. For example, the certificate may state that the costs are limited to a certain amount. It may be necessary at some stage to amend the certificate to increase the amount of cover. If this is overlooked the Solicitor may find that there is a shortfall of costs payable by the Legal Aid Agency. The client file should be marked in such a way that any amendments needed are clearly set out.

- **Computers**

Almost all firms now work with the help of computers. Case management systems assist in the keeping of an efficient and effective file. Many law firms still have limited paper files. Some family departments operate a 'paper light' policy or even 'paper free'.

- **Keeping Accounts**

There are several reasons to keep books and records:

i. **Protection of the Public:** The minimum requirements are aimed at protection of the public. Records of money received from each client, what money paid out for each client, and what the unexpended balance is for each client.

ii. **For Decision Making:** But the most important reason to keep books and records is because it is in the firm's best interest. By maintaining complete, accurate and up to date records, it will have current financial information available to make sound financial decisions about the practice.

iii. **Meeting Statutory Obligations:** Proper accounting records also help meet the statutory obligations in filing reports on time to the tax authorities for income tax and to other law related associations and regulators.

- Law firms practise under the strict rules of the Solicitors Regulations. All fee earners running a family law file must be familiar with the basic rules of how solicitors accounts work.

- It is important to know that a law firm with have at least two bank accounts. The first is the Office account and the second is the Client account. The Office account is owned by those who run the firm and the Client account is owned by the clients. The contents of each account must not mix with the other. They should be kept entirely separate from each other.

- Practically speaking, payment from a client account should only take place if the client in question has deposited a sum of money to cover that expense. Otherwise, payment for that expense must be paid out of the Office account.

- Fee earners must be familiar with terms such as profit costs and disbursements. Profit costs are the amount your firm is charging the client excluding VAT and disbursements are expenses paid out on behalf of a client such as court fees.

- **Solicitors Regulation Authority (SRA) Accounts Rules**

The SRA Accounts Rules set out requirements for client money and client accounts, dealing with other money belonging to clients or third parties, and accountants' reports and storage and retention of accounting records. The rules apply to all firms regulated by the SRA, including all those who manage or work within such firms. Firms will need to have systems and controls in place to ensure compliance with these rules.

A law firm has a responsibility to:

i. Protect client money

ii. Act with integrity

iii. Behave in a way that maintains the trust the public places in the solicitor and in the provision of legal services

iv. Comply with legal and regulatory obligations and deal with regulators in an open and cooperative manner

v. Run the business or carry out a role in the business effectively and in accordance with proper governance and sound financial and risk management principles.

https://www.sra.org.uk/solicitors/standards-regulations/

- **Funding the case**

A law firm is a business with a view to making a profit. Fees are charged to the client for work done and by agreement with the client. The charge can vary between solicitors but most charge on an hourly rate. Bills are rendered periodically and the client is responsible for payment. Some law firms charge on a fixed fee basis. Clients are often asked to pay a sum of money in advance of any work being done to cover future fees. This is paid 'on account of costs'

The level of fees is set out in the client care letter delivered to the client before work commences. This letter should also give the client an estimate of future costs. Interim bills can be rendered part way through a case. A bill rendered at the end of the case is called a Final bill which is an indication that the file will be closed once payment has been made by the client. More details can be found in Chapter 10.

- **Closing a file**

When work has been completed and the final bill has been paid, the Solicitor will take steps to close the file. He/she will write to the client confirming the outcome of the case and inform the client that the file will be stored for future reference. The closed file will be kept for a set period of time and then destroyed. The file is available to the client until then. More details can be found in Chapter 11.

https://www.lawsociety.org.uk/en/topics/business-management/file-closure-management

- **Finally**

You will see that the content of a family file is vitally important. If time and attention is given to the matters covered in this chapter it will go some way to keeping an efficient and orderly file. It will also help to keep a client happy and satisfied that they have been given a good legal service during what is often a difficult time in their life. Most importantly, the file must be handled in accordance with the professional rules governing the fee earner in question.

https://www.sra.org.uk/solicitors/standards-regulations/code-conduct-solicitors/

CHAPTER 10

FUNDING A FAMILY LAW CASE

Introduction

a. At the outset of a case, usually during the first interview, the solicitor will discuss with the client the question of how the case is going to be paid for. The solicitor must send the client the terms of business, including costs, of the firm. This is usually in a separate letter (often referred to as client care letter) and sent in duplicate, requiring the client to sign and return one copy, which should be placed on the client's file.

b. It is the duty of the solicitor to update the client throughout the case as to the fees which have been incurred and are likely to be incurred. Interim bills can be sent out as the case progresses to cover the ongoing work of the solicitor.

c. Solicitors often require money to be paid into their client account to cover any outgoings which they may incur on their client's behalf such as the court fees for issuing a divorce petition.

Methods of funding cases

- **The Hourly Rate** is the main way in which lawyers are paid for their work in family cases. Charging rates are set by the firm and vary according to location and seniority of the Solicitor dealing with the case.

- **Deferred Payment of Legal Fees**, also called *Sears Tooth* agreements can be entered into whereby lawyers can opt to wait

- until a case is finalised before requiring payment. Deferred payments are likely to be available only where there is insufficient income to meet the lawyer's fees but there is sufficient capital, which once unlocked, can pay the fees.

- **Court Orders** can also be used to secure payment of lawyers' fees, which is dealt with under ss 49–54 Legal Aid, Sentencing and Punishment of Offenders Act 2012 which allows the court to order a party to make payment to their former spouse or civil partner for their legal costs, which will be known as a Legal Services Payment Order (LSPO). This type of order under s22ZA Matrimonial Causes Act 1973 is available in proceedings for divorce/dissolution/(judicial) separation and in connected financial relief proceedings.

- **Funded by loans** where there is no other way of funding a case. Specialist family litigation loans are available to fund family cases. (**https://www.ifa-direct.com**).

- **Other Funding Options.** Fixed-fees are becoming more widespread in family cases. It used to be the situation that only initial interviews were conducted on a fixed-fee bases but now clients can secure fixed-fees for each element of their case. This is becoming more common as clients are choosing to do a lot of the routine work themselves (such as preparing their own financial statements), only requiring the Solicitor to do certain elements of the case. This practice called "unbundling".

- **Legal Aid**

Legal aid available for a limited range of family cases including:

- domestic abuse cases under Part IV of the Family Law Act 1996

- private family cases where there is evidence of domestic abuse

- public family law proceedings regarding the protection of children

- representation for children who are made parties to private family proceedings

- wardship

- child abduction

- forced marriage protection order proceedings

- legal advice in support of mediation

For those clients eligible for legal aid, they must pass both a means and a merits test. This means their financial position will be looked at. Those in receipt of certain welfare benefits will automatically be eligible under the means test. The merits test asks if there is "sufficient benefit" to the client being allowed legal advice. This ensures that advice is not given on trivial matters. To qualify for legal aid on the basis that the applicant or their child(ren) has been the victim of domestic abuse or violence and evidence must be provided. **Civil Legal Aid (Procedure) (Amendment) (No 2) Regulations 2017, SI 2017/1237**

Statutory charge

The statutory charge is the means by which costs payable out of the legal aid fund in relation to proceedings under which money or property has been recovered or preserved are repaid to the fund. A solicitor is under a duty to protect the legal aid fund and no monies can be paid to the client in respect of any costs, lump sum or sale proceeds ordered (or agreed) to be paid to the client, or any other capital recovered or preserved by court order or agreement. Sufficient monies must be retained by the solicitor to cover the full amount of the statutory charge.

Legal Aid, Sentencing and Punishment of Offenders Act 2012, Sch 1, Pt 1

Civil Legal Aid (Procedure) Regulations 2012, SI 2012/3098, regs 4–10

Civil Legal Aid (Merits Criteria) Regulations 2013, SI 2013/104, SI 2013/104

https://www.gov.uk/government/organisations/legal-aid-agency

CHAPTER 11

CLOSING A FAMILY LAW FILE

File closure as an integral part of your processes and procedures for ongoing systematic file management. Good file management from the outset of a matter will enable effective, efficient, and prompt file closure at its end.

The **SRA Standards and Regulations 2019** is the primary authority on this subject which should be consulted for further information and clarification.

The importance of a clear system

- A systematic approach will increase efficiency by reducing clutter and cutting down on difficulties in retrieving files. This will help mitigate the risk of not being able to properly identify and assess work in progress, and of regulatory non-compliance and/or negligence.

- In relation to individual matters, there are specific file-related risks which can be mitigated by:

    - ensuring that documents and other assets entrusted to the firm are properly stored and safeguarded

    - ensuring that the matter has been billed, all monies paid, and that all ledgers are clear

    - informing the client that the matter is now closed

- informing the client about any future action required

- informing the client how long you will retain their file for, how they can retrieve the files and of any associated costs

Client confidentiality

It is a legal and regulatory requirement to ensure that client confidentiality is protected. This duty continues after the conclusion of your client's matter. You must also ensure confidentiality when closing and storing files.

File closure policy and checklist

- A law firm should have a written, standardised policy for file closure.

- Unless there are compelling exceptional reasons to the contrary, you should ensure that a file is fully closed promptly and in accordance with your policy once you are satisfied that all issues relating to the matter have been concluded. It is suggested that where there are still actions that need to be taken, the client is not informed that the retainer is ended until these actions have been taken.

- A checklist that accords with your policy will help to preserve a consistent approach. It should be used and completed on every file closure and retained on the file after being signed off. The contents of your checklist will vary depending upon your firm's policies, processes and procedures, and whether your files are maintained in a paper or digital format or a combination of both.

- You should consider whether to include the following matters and to check that:

- the client's objectives have been achieved and all related administrative work has been fully completed, including any issues and/or complaints raised by the client

  - if required, a report is made to the client on any further action they are required to take in the matter and what (if anything) your firm will do

  - the file has been maintained in an orderly manner in accordance with your procedures and all the papers, file and attendance notes, and drafts are correctly and sequentially marked and identifiable

  - any original documentation or other property belonging to the client is returned (save for items which are by agreement to be stored by the practice), duplicate papers and emails removed whenever possible, and correspondence stored in date order

  - all transactions have been completed and/or registered

  - the final bill has been forwarded to the client, or other party, and has been paid. All outstanding disbursements and administrative charges have been paid and any other outstanding monies have been agreed to be written off by the firm

  - the accounts ledgers are clear and you have accounted to the client for any outstanding money

  - any undertakings have been discharged and the discharge recorded. A final risk review has been carried out and any identified further action has been undertaken

- if necessary, contact has been made with the firm's professional indemnity insurers

- any agreement made with the client to use the matter for publicity purposes has been signed off

- administration has been completed for archiving and recording the date for destruction of documents where appropriate

- if appropriate, the client has been advised about arrangements for storage and retrieval of papers (and associated costs) and other items retained and any charges to be made in this regard

- In particular, on closure you should check that at the conclusion of the matter you:

- reported the outcome of the matter to the client and explained any further action that they or the firm are required still to take

- maintained a copy of the closing letter on the file

- where appropriate, advised the client about arrangements for storage, destruction and retrieval of papers, and any related charges (unless this has already been agreed in the terms of business)

- if required, advised the client when the matter should be further reviewed

Electronic filing

- Files may be paper-based, maintained in an electronic case management system or may be a hybrid of the two.

- If you intend to store documents in an electronic format, you should first consider whether the absence of paper documents will be detrimental to the client's interests before you agree such storage methods with your client.

- You should also consider any file retention requirements of your professional indemnity insurers when assessing the appropriate length of time to retain files.

- Increasing amounts of data are stored digitally. Emails, in particular, may be stored digitally, even if there are paper-based files. In addition, incoming letters, documents and other papers are increasingly scanned and filed digitally. Files are now frequently scanned when the paper copy file is closed and destroyed.

- You should ensure that you identify and take appropriate steps to mitigate the risks associated with the storage of data in an electronic filing system and in accordance with the **Data Protection Act 2018**, and that your policies and procedures for file closure include all digitally-stored data. In particular, throughout the life of the file and upon closure you should consider the following:

    - securely storing the digital data relating to the file in specified locations and ensuring that the data is fully backed up

    - ensuring that your clients' details (for example, address) are updated

- making sure that your systems have sufficient capacity to accommodate and manage the amount of data to be stored

- You may need to delete digitally stored data on closure of the file. In these circumstances, you should take into account the fact that the deletion of electronic files from a hard drive is not as straightforward as the destruction of paper files. There are forensic tools with which "deleted" data can be retrieved and accessed. Your records management policy should therefore make provision for the "scrubbing" of data, where appropriate, so that destruction and storage of electronic files is consistent with the management of your paper records. It is also worth noting that, under the **Data Protection Act 2018**, individuals have a right to have personal data erased.

- Individuals also have rights to prevent processing in specific circumstances, such as where the personal data is no longer necessary in relation to the purpose for which it was originally collected/processed, or when the individual withdraws consent. You should also consider breach of security and confidentiality risks specifically associated with the storage of digital data. In particular, computer networks and servers can be compromised and confidential information may be stolen. In addition, viruses can infiltrate networks, servers and backup tapes, erasing firm and client information. You should therefore ensure that you have appropriate technical and organisational measures in place ("the security principle").

- You should also keep in mind that the **Data Protection Act 2018** stipulates the need to notify the Information Commissioner (ICO) of a breach where it is likely to result in a risk to the rights and freedoms of individuals. There is also a need to notify the individuals if a breach is likely to result in a high risk to the rights and freedoms of individuals.

Outsourcing

You should consider whether you outsource any activities that could have an impact on your policies and procedures for file closure.

Accounts

- Your policies and procedures for file closure should include provision for the closure of the file within your accounts system. You should ensure that such provisions fully comply with the SRA Accounts Rules.

- Your procedures should ensure that a file is not closed where:

    - there is a credit/debit balance in the office or client accounts

    - there is a 'work in progress' balance yet to be invoiced or written off

    - there is an outstanding bill

    - interest is yet to be paid to the client

- The procedure should also allocate responsibility for dealing with these outstanding issues and finalising the closure of the file upon their resolution.

Retention of Files

- There is no specific Law Society guidance stating how long a file should be retained in storage. Firms therefore need to decide how long they wish to store closed files taking into account relevant statutory provisions such as limitation periods.

- Many solicitors view the minimum period that any file should be kept for as six years, the primary limitation period under the Limitation Act 1980. Most claims are made within this period. In family cases files are often retained until the clients' youngest child attains the age of 18 years.

- In your client closure letter, you should advise the client how long you will retain the file and outline what will happen to the file after that time. You should also advise the client of any costs relating to any of the following:

    - Storage

    - Retrieval

    - additional copies of papers requested by the client.

Closure of a law firm

- When the SRA closes down a firm, funds are arranged to be transferred to the SRA and an intervention agent (another firm of solicitors) will be asked to hold the firm's papers safely. These will include clients' deeds, documents, case files and papers. The intervention agent will try and contact all the clients and ask what they want done with their papers although they may not be able to do that immediately.

- A client or former client of a practice which has closed down should contact the intervention agent and consider instructing another firm of solicitors to act on your behalf going forward. This is especially important if your case is urgent.

https://www.lawsociety.org.uk/topics/business-management/closing-down-your-practice-regulatory-requirements#legal-status

PART B

ORDERS

CHAPTER 12

COMMON FAMILY COURT ORDERS

Specific Issue Order

A Specific Issue Order is a court order that is used when people with Parental Responsibility for a child disagree on a particular matter, such as what a child's surname should be after divorce.

As someone with Parental Responsibility, you are allowed to have a say on a child's upbringing. If those with Parental Responsibility have opposing views on a certain subject, a Specific Issue Order can be applied for. The Court will then consider what is in the child's best interests and make the decision about that particular issue.

For example, a Specific Issue Order may deal with:

- How a child should be educated

- What medical treatment a child should receive

- A child's religious upbringing

- Whether a child can be taken outside of England & Wales

- Changing a child's name or surname.

Prohibited Steps Order

A Prohibited Steps Order is a court order that prevents someone from exercising their powers of Parental Responsibility, meaning they can't do particular things eg remove a child from the country.

Those with Parental Responsibility have a right to make decisions about a child's upbringing. If others with Parental Responsibility disagree with another parent's actions (or proposed actions) and want to stop it happening, a Prohibited Steps Order can be applied for. If successful, this will remove that individual's right to act.

For example, a Prohibited Steps Order may:

- Prevent a parent from taking a child out of the country

- Prevent a parent from changing a child's surname

- Prevent a parent from relocating with a child

- Prevent the child from receiving certain medical treatment.

Child Arrangements Order

A Child Arrangements Order was previously known as a Residence Order. This court order sets out the living arrangements for a child or children, including which parent the child/children will live with for the majority of the time.

A Child Arrangements Order will be needed if it cannot be decided with whom a child should live. In these cases the court will make a decision based on what is in the child's best interest. The parent with whom the child lives for most of the time is known as the 'Resident Parent', and he/she is responsible for making day-to-day decisions about the child's upbringing.

For example, a Child Arrangements Order can deal with:

- Which parent the child will live with

- How much time the child will spend with the other parent (if any)

- When a child will spend time with the other parent

- Whether contact with the other parent should be supervised.

Non-molestation Orders

A Non-molestation Order is a court injunction. It can be used to prevent a partner or ex-partner from displaying violent or threatening behaviour towards the other partner and their children. This includes intimidation, pestering and harassment.

If there is a risk of domestic violence and a fear for the safety of a partner and/or their children, a Non-molestation Order should be applied for without delay. A Non-Molestation Order can be adapted to individual circumstances to ensure that a partner is protected.

For example, a Non-molestation Order may stop a particular person:

- Being on the same road as a home or child's school

- Contacting the partner or children

- Damaging property

- Communicating with a partner other than through a third party.

Occupation Orders

An **Occupation Order** is a court injunction. It can be used to control who lives in the family home. It can also restrict a particular person from entering the area surrounding the family home.

Occupation Orders are often used alongside Non-molestation Orders. They help people who want to remain in the family home, but who are scared to do so because of the threat of domestic violence.

With an Occupation Order, a person can prevent a violent ex-partner from being in the property or coming near it, even if he/she is on the Tenancy Agreement or the mortgage.

Financial Applications

The Family Court can consider the financial position of couples who are divorcing. Family Courts have a wide range of powers to make financial orders, including the provision of periodical payments, lump sums, pension sharing, pension attachments, property adjustment, transfer and settlement of property, and a variation of settlements that have already been made.

Pension Sharing Orders

A Pension Sharing Order is a court order that rules how a pension pot should be split following divorce or civil partnership dissolution.

To enable this to happen, each person must disclose how much is in their pension pot (if they have one), and the court will then decide how it should be divided. A Judge will say how much a client should receive from your ex's pension, and how much he/she will receive from yours.

In England and Wales, the amount awarded will be expressed as a percentage of the transfer values. This can either be transferred into an existing pension, or a new pension can be created.

Maintenance Orders

A Maintenance Order is a court order that states how much spousal maintenance someone must pay their ex-husband/wife following divorce. This is different to child maintenance, which is dealt with separately.

The Court may order Spousal Maintenance to be paid if one person earns significantly less than the other, and needs additional money to ensure their needs are taken care of. Sometimes this happens where one person has given up work during the marriage in order to care for the children, so when the relationship breaks down, he/she has very little money or career prospects of their own.

For example, a Maintenance Order can state:

- How much money should be paid and how frequently i.e. £1,000 per month

- When Spousal Maintenance payments should stop.

Public law orders

There are several possible final orders the court can make:

- **Care Order:** Local Authority gain parental responsibility for the child and the child becomes looked-after until the age of 18 unless discharged before.

- **Supervision Order:** Local Authority is granted the power to monitor the child's needs whilst the child lives at home or elsewhere.

- **Special Guardianship Order:** An order that places a child or young person to live with someone other than their parent on a long-term basis.

- **Placement and Adoption Orders:** The court provides permission to the Local Authority to place a child for adoption even if the child's parents do not provide consent.

Cases about human fertilisation and embryology and surrogacy

The Human Fertilisation and Embryology Act 2008 governs cases about the legal parentage of children conceived through the use of donated sperm, eggs or embryos, for example by way of surrogacy. The Family

Court can make orders identifying a person as the parent of a child born by way of surrogacy.

Cases about forced marriage and female genital mutilation

Under the Family Law Act 1996 the court may make an order for the purposes of protecting a person from being forced into marriage, or from any attempt to force them into marriage, or an order protecting a person who has already been forced into marriage.

Under the Female Genital Mutilation Act 2003 the Family Courts can make a female genital mutilation protection order for the purposes of protecting a girl against the commission of a genital mutilation offence or protecting a girl against whom such an offence has been committed.

Cases under the Inherent Jurisdiction

In certain cases the Family Division of the High Court can still make a child a ward of court in order to protect the child. Under the inherent jurisdiction of the High Court, the court can also, for example, authorise medical treatment for a child or the withdrawal of medical treatment for a child where a dispute arises between the child's parents and treating doctors, or to restrain or permit publication regarding court proceedings.

CHAPTER 13

DIVORCE PROCEEDINGS

A client is able to obtain a divorce in England and Wales if he/she:

- has been married for at least one year;

- their marriage is legally recognised by UK law; and

- the relationship has permanently broken down

- Usually, one or both parties should be domiciled or resident in England and Wales, but even if that is not the case, the client may still be entitled to divorce here.

As of 6th April 2022, the 'no-fault' divorce laws are in effect. The rules are set out in the Family Procedure (Amendment) Rules 2022.

Under the Divorce, Dissolution and Separation Act 2020:

- Allows joint applications for divorce, civil partnership dissolution and judicial separation. Applicants can still apply on their own (a sole application).

- Ends the need to state one of the five facts or 'grounds' for divorce – adultery, behaviour, desertion, living apart for two or five years.

- Introduces a single requirement for a statement of 'irretrievable breakdown' of the relationship.

- Requires the respondent to a sole application to respond within 14 days.

- Removes the respondent's ability to dispute (formerly defend or contest) the divorce or dissolution.

- Only allows disputed divorce/dissolution on grounds of jurisdiction, validity of the marriage/partnership, or fraud and procedural non-compliance.

- Introduces a new minimum period of 20 weeks between the divorce application being issued and being able to apply for the conditional order (which replaces decree nisi).

- Does not change the current requirement of six weeks and one day between the conditional order and final order (previously decree absolute).

- One party can still apply for a divorce on their own if your spouse does not agree to the divorce or will not cooperate or respond to the court.

The Court Process

For those who are eligible to get a divorce in the UK, the process in England and Wales is as follows:

1. **Application**: Complete **a D8 application form** requesting a divorce or civil partnership dissolution. This can either be on a paper form sent by post or via the Gov.UK digital service online. Parties can apply themselves as a litigant in person or they can appoint a solicitor to act on their behalf.

2. **Sole or joint application:** The applicant will be asked whether the application is being made solely or jointly (with the full knowledge and participation of the spouse/civil partner). In a sole application, there will be an applicant and respondent. In a joint application, one party will be applicant 1 and the other will be applicant 2.

3. **Personal details:** As a sole applicant he/she will need to complete the details about themselves and the respondent. There is an option to keep the details confidential so that the respondent is not able to view his/her address and phone numbers, etc. On a joint application, both parties must fill in their own details.

4. **Details of the marriage:** There is a requirement to provide the marriage certificate or civil partnership certificate.

5. **Jurisdiction:** There is a need to prove that the parties are eligible to be divorced in England or Wales.

6. **Irretrievable breakdown:** The applicant(s) will need to state that he/she is seeking divorce or dissolution because the marriage/civil partnership has broken down irretrievably. This statement alone will enable the court to make the order for divorce or dissolution.

7. **Other matters:** There is a need to tell the court about previous matters relating to the marriage or civil partnership, such as child proceedings or a previous application for divorce/dissolution. There is a need to tell the court of any other orders the applicant(s) wish to apply for in relation to money, property, and/or children.

8. **Statement of Truth:** The statement of truth is the completion and signing of the application. In a joint application, applicant 2 will need to sign this as well.

9. **Serving the application:** A sole applicant can choose how they wish the respondent to receive the divorce application. The default method will be via email or by post if the respondent's email address is not known. If the applicant does not know the address of the respondent, he/she will need to complete form D11 which enables service via email alone. The applicant can arrange service of the application themselves

10. **Responding to an application:** Respondents to a sole application have 14 days to respond. They will complete a **D10 form**. Disputes on the grounds on grounds of jurisdiction, validity of the marriage/partnership, fraud or procedural non-compliance must be made on form D8B and submitted within 21 days of receiving the divorce/dissolution application.

11. **Apply for the Conditional Order:** After a minimum period of 20 weeks, the sole applicant can apply for the Conditional Order (formerly the decree nisi). Joint applicants must also wait 20 weeks. This period of time can be used to help the parties reflect on whether ending their relationship is the right course of action and also provides time for the parties to attempt to work out other issues such as arrangements for children and finances.

12. **Apply for the Final Order:** Once the Conditional Order has been granted, applicants, either solely or jointly, will need to wait six weeks and one day before they can apply for the Final Order. In sole applications, a 'notice of intention' must be served on the other party 14 days before the application for the Final Order is made.

13. **Granting of the Final Order:** Once the Final Order has been granted the marriage/civil partnership is officially dissolved and legal responsibility for the other party is at an end.

14. **The Court Fee** for divorce is currently £593 but this will increase over time.

CHAPTER 14

FINANCIAL APPLICATIONS

The Family Court can consider the financial position of couples who are divorcing. Family Courts have a wide range of powers to make financial orders, including the provision of periodical payments, lump sums, pension sharing, pension attachments, property adjustment, transfer and settlement of property, and a variation of settlements that have already been made. In some cases, the English and Welsh courts can deal with financial relief following an overseas divorce that is recognised in England and Wales, subject to certain conditions being met. In the majority of financial cases there are **three stages** to the court process:

1. **The First Directions Appointment (FDA)** is the first short hearing before a Judge. It usually lasts around 20-30 minutes. The aim is to make sure that both parties have provided all the information the court needs to decide on the value of the matrimonial assets both jointly and separately. The Judge can do a number of things at the FDA:

- Give directions about what needs to be done before a Judge can decide the case

- Decide which questions on any questionnaire the parties should each answer

- Decide whether the case needs the help of an expert to value an asset the parties cannot agree on, such as the family home or pension

- If the parties agree, make a final order

- Adjourn the proceedings for Mediation

- Treat the First Appointment as a Financial Dispute Resolution Appointment and indicate what order the court might make if the case goes on to a final hearing

- Fix a date for a Financial Dispute Resolution appointment

Advocates at the FDA should ensure the court has all the necessary information to make an order and explore the possibility of a settlement. If a settlement is reached, the advocate for the applicant will draft an order for consideration by the Judge.

Between the FDA and the next hearing

After the First Appointment, the parties should complete all tasks directed by the Judge at the First Directions Appointment by the deadlines given. This may include completing answers to each other's questionnaires, sending these answers to the court and a copy to each other and obtaining an expert's report on the value of the family home or a pension.

If the parties cannot reach an agreement, the court will expect them to make a proposal for settling their case before the Financial Dispute Resolution Appointment. The applicant should write to the court in advance of this hearing taking place, setting out what proposals he/she has made for reaching an agreement and what response has been received. If a party refuses to negotiate, the court can order him/her to pay some of the other party's legal costs.

2. Financial Dispute Resolution Hearing (FDR)

This is the second hearing. At this hearing the court is given a summary of each party's financial position and the District Judge is expected to give an indication as to what he/she believes the outcome should be if the case proceeds to a full hearing. The purpose of this is to allow for the parties to negotiate and reach an agreement. The court will not go into the finer details of the case but will focus on the 'big picture'. The court cannot make a final order at this hearing unless the parties arrive at an agreement between themselves. The parties will be given some time during the course of the day to discuss the Judge's indication to see if an agreement is possible. The Judge who sits at this hearing is not allowed to hear the final hearing. If the parties arrive at an agreement the Judge can make a consent order. If the parties cannot reach an agreement at this hearing, the court will usually give directions for a Final Hearing. Advocates at the FDR will be expected to make oral submissions on behalf of their client before the Judge gives his/her indication. If the parties are able to arrive at a settlement, the applicant's advocate will draft an order for approval by the Judge. If the parties cannot agree the terms of an order, the court will give directions for the final hearing and advocates will need to make representations to the Judge as to the nature of those directions for example, when the final hearing will take place, what witnesses will give evidence, and who will prepare the court bundle.

3. The Final Hearing

At the Final Hearing the court will hear evidence from both parties and make a final decision as to the outcome. The Judge listens to the evidence, hears speeches from both parties and decides what order should be made as to how the family assets should be divided. These orders are set out in a written court order and presented to the parties. Advocates at the Final hearing will be expected to present evidence, cross examine witnesses and make submissions to the court on behalf of their client. They will also advise the client on a possible appeal and, if necessary, seek the court's permission to appeal.

Consent Orders in Financial Applications

Parties can reach an agreement on financial matters amicably, and so can sign a Consent Order. Even if court proceedings have started, those involved can negotiate and reach an agreement, rather than the court having to make a decision on their behalf. This agreement can then be drafted into a *Consent Order*.

The court will expect there to have been full and frank disclosure of each party's financial circumstances. This information is set out within a *Statement of Information* which is sent to the court with a Consent Order. When considering a Consent Order, the court will look at whether the agreement reached is fair, and that there is appropriate financial provision for those involved. The court therefore has a discretionary approach, and does not have to endorse the Consent Order, even if it is agreed by both sides. If both parties have obtained independent legal advice, provided there is evidence of their financial circumstances and the proposed financial settlement is reasonable, it's likely that the Consent Order will be approved by the Judge.

The Consent Order itself can incorporate a number of sections:

- Recitals – agreements that have been reached between the parties which the court cannot order, but should be recorded on the Consent Order to provide clarification.

- Undertakings – promises that are made to the court, that if breached can be enforced by the court. These have to be signed by the person they apply to.

- Orders – these will include orders about property, money and pensions.

The basis of a Consent Order is often to cut the financial ties that spouses and civil partners have with each other. This will prevent either party making further claims in the future. This is known as a *Clean Break Order*. Once a consent order is approved by the court, it is very difficult to argue that the agreement reached is not appropriate or fair.

Requirements for a Consent Order

In order to approve a Consent Order without a contested hearing, the court requires certain information. This enables the court to make a Consent Order without full investigation and oral evidence. This information is prescribed in *Rule 9.26 of the Family Procedure Rules 2010*.

(a) The applicant files: **Form A Notice of Intention to Proceed** with an application for a Financial Order; two copies of a draft of the order sought, one copy endorsed with a statement signed by the respondent to the application signifying agreement. Each party must file with the court and serve on the other party a Statement of Information (**Form D81**) Where each party's Statement of Information is contained in one form, it must be signed by both the applicant and the respondent to certify that they have read the contents of the other party's statement. Where each party's Statement of Information is in a separate form, the form of each party must be signed by the other party to certify that they have read the contents of the statement contained in that form. A court fee is payable on the filing of the application

(b) Unless the court directs otherwise, the applicant and the respondent need not attend the hearing of an application for a Consent Order. Where all or any of the parties attend the hearing of a financial application, the court may dispense with the filing of a Statement of Information. If the Consent order is to vary periodical payments or for interim periodical payments, only information as to net income will be required. However, some

District Judges may require information about capital at the time of the variation of periodical payments.

Court hearings:
Finance

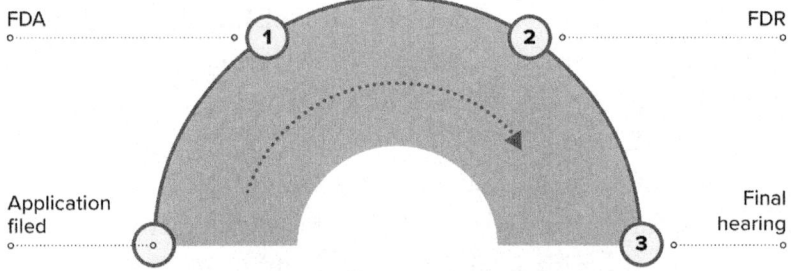

CHAPTER 15

PRIVATE CHILDREN APPLICATIONS

Under the Children Act 1989 the Family Court has jurisdiction to make child arrangement orders in proceedings between the parents of a child where the parents do not agree on issues such as with whom the child should live, how much contact should take place, which school the child should go to or whether they can move to live abroad with one of their parents. The cases can also involve grandparents and other relatives. These are known as 'private law' children cases.

Private Law cases are brought by private individuals, generally in connection with divorce or the parents' separation. Orders include: parental responsibility, financial applications, special guardianship orders, and orders under Section 8 of the Children Act 1989.

Practice Direction 12B The Child Arrangements Programme (CAP) is made up of 23 paragraphs that give a full picture of how the court process should work. This document is readily available on the internet.

The court procedure in Children Act proceedings can vary depending upon the particular application being made and the circumstances of the case, but the most common will be as follows:

1. First Hearing and Dispute Resolution Appointment (FHDRA)

This is the first court hearing after an application has been made to court in private family law proceedings. **Form C100** is the usual form of application.

The FHDRA is held to assist the court in identifying issues between the parties at an early stage and to see if it is possible for the parties to reach an agreement. A Cafcass Officer will often be present.

The Judge or Lay Magistrates and the Cafcass Officer will attempt to assist the parties to reach agreement. Sometimes, there will be a Mediator in the court building who might also assist the parties, and if the parties have not yet attempted mediation, the court may order that they do so before court proceedings commence.

Prior to the hearing, Cafcass should have prepared a *Schedule 2 Letter*, sometimes known as a *Safeguarding Letter*, which should be shared with both parties, unless doing so would put either party or the children at risk and/or the document contains information which is sensitive and of which the other party is unaware.

The Schedule 2 Letter will include background checks on the parties. These checks will include enquiries with the Local Authority and the Police as to any relevant information. Cafcass will have spoken to the parties over the telephone to ascertain their views on the application. The Schedule 2 letter usually gives the court guidance as to what steps should be taken to progress the application.

If the parties can reach agreement at the FHDRA, a final order may be made setting out the details of the agreement if the court deems it to be in the children's best interests. If the parties cannot reach agreement, the court will seek to determine the areas where they disagree and the reasons why.

If the case concerns contact and/or residence and serious allegations are made, the court may decide not to permit contact while matters are investigated. The Judge or Lay Magistrates and Cafcass may propose that contact should be supervised or that contact takes place at a Contact Centre while matters are investigated. If there are no serious concerns, the court may order that there should be contact immediately, pending a final order at a future hearing.

Case management decisions considered at the FHDRA include:

- Issues that are agreed and the key issues to be determined

- Whether the matter should be listed for a fact-finding hearing

- Whether any interim orders which can usefully be made e.g. indirect, supported or supervised contact pending a Dispute Resolution Appointment or Final hearing

- What directions are required to ensure the application is ready for a Dispute Resolution Appointment or Final hearing including statements or reports. In particular, whether the court should order a S7 report and the issues to be addressed in the report.

- Whether the application should be listed for a Dispute Resolution Appointment or even a Final Hearing.

Advocates need to prepare carefully for the court hearing and take an active role at the hearing itself. If the parties are able to arrive at an agreement the applicant's advocate will draft an order for approval by the Judge or Lay Magistrates. If the parties cannot agree the terms of an order, the court will give directions for the next hearing. Advocates will need to make representations to the Judge or Lay Magistrates as to the nature of those directions.

2. Dispute Resolution Appointment (DRA)

This is the second hearing when the court will try to narrow the issues in the case, consider any expert evidence (including any S7 report from Cafcass or the Local Authority that has been filed) and decide whether there is a need for a Fact Finding Hearing. Courts use this hearing as an opportunity to resolve matters without the need for a full hearing.

At the DRA the court will:

- identify the key issues to be determined and the extent to which those issues can be resolved or narrowed

- consider whether the DRA can be used as a final hearing

- identify the evidence to be heard on the issues which remain to be resolved at the final hearing

- give final case management directions including:

- filing of further evidence

- filing of a statement of facts/issues remaining to be determined;

- filing of a witness template and/or skeleton arguments

- ensuring compliance with Practice Direction 27A regarding court bundles

- listing the case for a Final Hearing.

No evidence is called at the DRA unless the court has made an earlier direction.

Advocates need to be prepared for the DRA hearing and take an active role in attempting to arrive at an agreement. If the parties are able to arrive at an agreement, the applicant's advocate will draft an order for approval by the Judge or Lay Magistrates. If the parties cannot agree the terms of an order, the court will give directions for a Final Hearing. Advocates will need to make representations to the Judge or Lay Magistrates as to the nature of those directions.

3. Fact Finding Hearing

A Fact Finding Hearing is a court hearing that considers the evidence surrounding any serious allegations made by one party against the other. Evidence is heard, which will normally include parties being cross-examined. After having heard the evidence, the Judge or Lay Magistrates will decide whether the alleged incidents happened or not. Most commonly, these allegations concern domestic abuse. Domestic abuse includes neglect, emotional and physical harm and violence. It is for the party making the allegations to prove that they are true. The Judge or Lay Magistrates will consider on the balance of probabilities whether the allegations are true or not.

In preparation for a Fact Finding Hearing the party making the allegations will be asked to provide a list of the allegations to the court in the form of a *Scott Schedule*. The party against whom the allegations are made will be directed to respond to the allegations within a set time frame. Both parties will be ordered to make written statements setting out their accounts of the allegations. Witnesses can also make a statement and give evidence with the court's permission. The court will often place a limit on the number of allegations to be included in the schedule of allegations to ensure that the case is manageable and the fact finding hearing is focused on the most relevant issues.

Advocates will be expected to present their client's case, cross examine witnesses and make submissions to the court. See Chapter 14 for more details on Finding of Fact hearings and in particular the importance of *Practice Direction 12J Child Arrangements & Contact Orders: Domestic Abuse and Harm*

4. Final Hearing

At a Final Hearing, the Judge or Lay Magistrates will consider all of the evidence of the parties and any Cafcass or Local Authority report. If there has been a Fact Finding hearing the Judge will take into account any findings made in the course of those proceedings. Using all of this information, the Judge or Lay Magistrates will assess the evidence and come to a decision guided by the Welfare Check List. Advocates will be expected to present the client's case, cross examine witnesses and make submissions to the court. The applicant will have prepared a court bundle, agreed the content with the respondent and filed copies with the court. This court bundle will form the basis of any court hearing. See chapter 13 for more details.

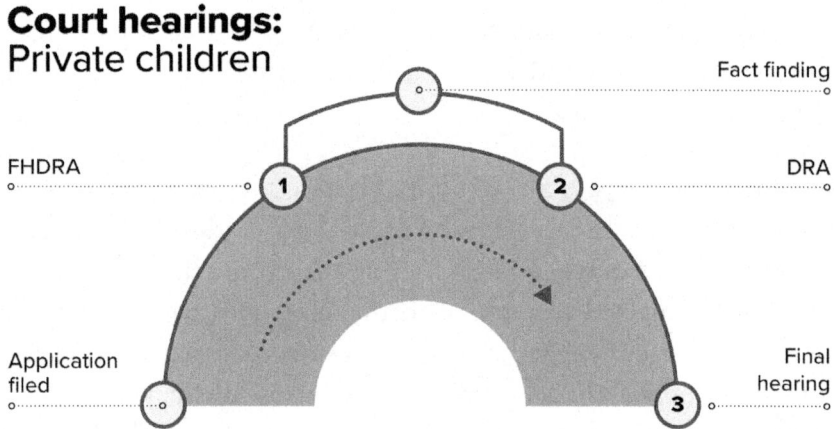

Court hearings:
Private children

- FHDRA
- Fact finding
- DRA
- Application filed
- Final hearing

CHAPTER 16

PUBLIC LAW CHILDREN APPLICATIONS

Cases about protecting children

Under the Children Act 1989, the court can make public law orders in proceedings between a local authority, the parents of the child and the child, placing the child under the supervision of the local authority or placing the child in the care of the local authority. These orders are made to protect the child where the child has suffered, or is at risk of suffering, significant harm. Before making such public law orders, the court must be satisfied that they are in the child's best interests and necessary and proportionate.

Public law cases are brought by Local Authorities or an authorised person (currently only the NSPCC) where an application is made for a Care Order or Supervision Order in respect of a child.

If Social Services believe a child is at risk of significant harm, they can apply to court for permission to take action to protect the child. This will give parental responsibility for the child concerned to the Local Authority applying for the Care order. The Local Authority can also apply for a Supervision Order which places the child under the Supervision of the Local Authority. An Emergency Protection Order is a further order which is used to ensure the immediate safety of a child by taking him/her to a place of safety, or by preventing their removal from a place of safety.

Many hearings take place at short notice and involve the advocates in negotiations, submissions and even cross examination at an early stage in the proceedings.

In proceedings under *Section 31 of the Children Act 1989* the child's parents and anyone else who holds parental responsibility for the child will be a party to the proceedings. They have a right to attend each court hearing and to have access to all reports and evidence filed with the court. They also have the right to legal representation paid for by legal aid free of any charge. The child has separate legal representation and the assistance of a Cafcass Guardian.

Practice Direction 12A describes the court process in cases of public law care proceedings. *Section 14(2) of the Children and Families Act 2014* amended *s.32(1)(a) of the Children Act 1989* to insert that a case must be concluded without delay and, in any event, *within 26 weeks,* beginning with the day on which the application was issued.

Interim Care Orders

If Social Services are of the view that a child needs to be removed from the care of the parents before the final hearing, the social worker in the case will seek an Interim Care Order. The parties in the proceedings will be requested to attend a court hearing to put forward representations. At this court hearing the court will decide:

- Whether to grant an Interim Care Order

- With whom the child should live with until the final hearing

- Who will have contact with the child until the final hearing

If the court agrees, the Local Authority can take the child into care on a temporary basis initially for up to 8 weeks. This can be extended by permission of the court.

Case Management Hearings

The Case Management Hearing is a court hearing where directions will be made as to how to progress the proceedings. The court gives detailed Case Management directions, including:

- Identifying the key issues

- Identifying the evidence necessary to enable the court to resolve the key issues

- Deciding whether there is a real issue as to threshold to be resolved

This is generally a short hearing which will resolve procedural matters which enables the case to be ready for a final hearing.

Advocates for all parties will work together to bring about an agreement or prepare directions as to any future hearing. A draft order should be prepared, usually by the Local Authority, for the court to consider and approve.

Issues Resolution Hearings

The purpose of this hearing is to decide on whether the care proceedings can be concluded early. If this is not possible, the hearing will identify and narrow down the issues for determination at a final hearing:

- The court identifies the key issues to be determined and the extent to which those issues can be resolved or narrowed down at the IRH.

- The court considers whether the IRH can be used as a final hearing.

- The court resolves or narrows the issues by hearing evidence.

- The court identifies the evidence to be heard on the issues which remain to be resolved at the final hearing.

- The court gives final case management directions.

Advocates will work together to bring about an agreement or prepare directions as to any future hearing. A draft order should be prepared, usually by the Local Authority, for the court to consider and approve.

Final Hearings

If the child's parents, the Children's Guardian and the child's social workers are unable to agree a plan regarding the child, the case will proceed to a final hearing. The court will determine whether a Care Order or a Supervision Order is required to safeguard the welfare of the child. If the court agrees that a court order is necessary given the circumstances, final decisions will be made regarding with whom the child will live and contact arrangements for the parents and wider family. There are several possible final orders the court can make:

- **Care Order:** Local Authority gain parental responsibility for the child and the child becomes looked-after until the age of 18 unless discharged before.

- **Supervision Order:** Local Authority is granted the power to monitor the child's needs whilst the child lives at home or elsewhere.

- **Special Guardianship Order:** An order that places a child or young person to live with someone other than their parent on a long-term basis.

- **Placement and Adoption Orders:** The court provides permission to the Local Authority to place a child for adoption even if the child's parents do not provide consent. Most parties, including the child, in care proceedings will be legally represented by an experienced advocate.

Advocates should ensure that their client's case is put to the court at each stage of the proceedings including the court hearings. Negotiations and discussions frequently take place between the parties at and between each court hearing in an attempt to agree legal and procedural issues. In the event of a dispute on such matters, the court will be asked to adjudicate on the issues following representations by all the party's advocates. Parties are not usually expected to give evidence until the final hearing and only if the proceedings are contested. The court may hear evidence from the parties, experts, social workers, the Children's Guardian.

Court hearings:
Care proceedings

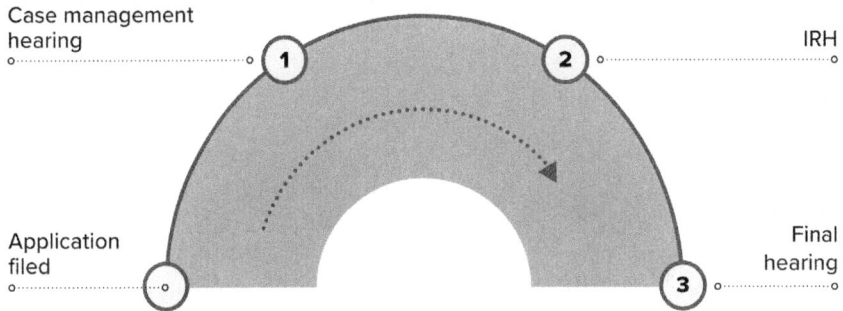

CHAPTER 17

DOMESTIC ABUSE INJUNCTIONS

Under the Family Law Act 1996 the court can make a non-molestation order preventing one person using violence or harassing another person where all the circumstances of the case, including the need to secure the health, safety and wellbeing of the applicant or any relevant child, require it. In these cases, the court can also make orders to stop coercive and controlling behaviour. The Domestic Abuse Act 2021 creates a statutory definition of domestic abuse and emphasises that domestic abuse is not just physical violence, but can also be emotional, controlling or coercive behaviour and economic abuse. The court can also make orders to stop coercive and controlling behaviour. There are two main types of injunctions under *Part IV Family Law Act 1996*: A Non-molestation Order and an Occupation Order.

Non-molestation Order

This Order aims to prevent a current or former partner/spouse from threatening or using violence against an applicant or a child. The order also aims to stop any harassing or intimidating behaviour. Its ultimate purpose is to protect the health, safety and well-being of the applicant, as well as that of their children. To apply for an injunction, the applicant must be an *'associated person'*. This means the applicant and respondent must be connected with each other in at least one of the following ways:

- they are or were married to each other

- they are or were in a civil partnership

- they live with each other or used to live together

- they live or used to live in the same household

- they are blood relations

- they are engaged to be married to each other even if the engagement ends

- they have children together – this may include those who are parents of the same child, as well as those who have parental responsibility for the same child

- they are in an 'intimate relationship of significant duration'

- they are both taking part in the same family proceedings e.g. children or divorce.

The Domestic Violence Crime and Victims Act 2004 amended the Family Law Act to include same sex couples. This means that people who live together are able to apply for Occupation Orders and Non-molestation Orders, regardless of gender or sexual orientation.

An Occupation Order

This order deals with issues as to who lives at the family home and can:

- order the abuser to move out of the home or to stay away from the home

- order the abuser to keep a certain distance away from the home

- order the abuser to stay in certain parts of the home at certain times, for example it can order him/her to sleep in a different bedroom

- order the abuser to allow the applicant back into the home if he/her has locked the applicant out

- order him/her to continue to pay the mortgage, rent or bills

When deciding whether to grant an Occupation Order the court will consider a number of factors including:

- the housing needs and resources of the applicant, the abuser and any children

- the financial resources of the parties

- the likely effect any order, or not making an order, will have on the applicant, the abuser and any child

- the applicant and the abuser's behaviour to one another

The court may also look at the harm that the applicant and any children might suffer if the order is not granted and the harm that the abuser and any child might suffer if an order is made.

The court can make both a Non-molestation Order and an Occupation Order if the court considers it is appropriate.

Those who can be protected by an injunction include the applicant and any relevant child. A relevant child is any child under 18:

- who is living or might be expected to live with the applicant or the abuser

- who is the subject of Family Court proceedings linked to an application for a Domestic Violence injunction; or

- whose interests the court thinks relevant

- If the child is over 18, or another adult family member needs protection, they will have to make their own application for an injunction.

Court hearings:
Injunctions

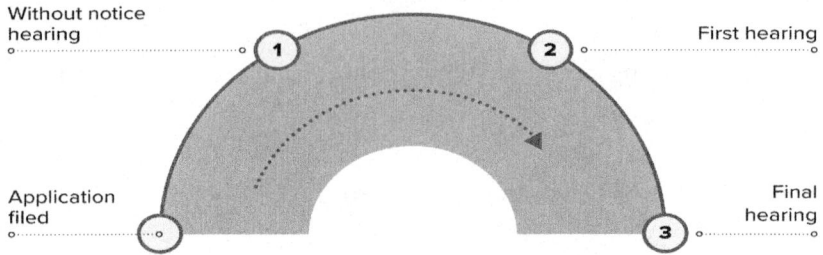

The application process

An application for a Non-molestation Order and/or an Occupation Order is made in the Family Court. The application form is *FL401*. There is no court fee for applying for a Domestic Violence Injunction. A witness statement should be filed giving details of the applicant's relationship with the respondent, any relevant children, past history of violence and the events which led to the making of an application and the order being sought.

Without Notice Hearing

If the injunction is urgent or the abuser could cause further harm if he/she is aware of the court application, the application can be made without notice to the respondent. In this case, the court can consider the application without the respondent being served or present at court. The court will have to be persuaded that there are good reasons to make an order urgently and in the absence of the respondent, which should be set out in the witness statement. Supporting documents from the Police or a doctor can help and should be attached as an exhibit to the witness statement.

If an order is granted without notice to the respondent, the court will set another hearing date to give the respondent an opportunity to put forward his/her response to the application.

The applicant will have to attend this hearing and may have to give evidence. The court will consider all the evidence and decide whether the order should be extended or varied.

As an alternative to an *Order*, the court may accept accept an *Undertaking* from the respondent. An Undertaking is a binding promise which the respondent makes to the court. It can be offered in lieu of a court order. In domestic abuse proceedings, an Undertaking is a promise to do or to avoid all the steps contemplated by the proposed court order. This means that the respondent agrees to observe these stipulations, but it is not a court order. Although an Undertaking is not a court order, it is still enforceable.

If respondent fails to honour his/her promise, then the applicant can seek to commit the respondent to prison for contempt of court. This is done by lodging an application for committal to prison, with an affidavit, listing details of the breach. If the court is satisfied the respondent has breached the Undertaking, it can deal with the matter by imposing:

a) Imprisonment for up to 2 years

b) Suspended sentence of imprisonment

c) An unlimited fine.

An Undertaking can only be made with the consent of the respondent.

An Undertaking should only be offered if he/she has genuinely behaved in a sufficiently threatening or unreasonable fashion. This does not mean that the respondent has to accept all the matters alleged against him/her but can be based on the respondent's own version of events. It is important that the respondent does not to agree to an Undertaking simply to avoid the case proceeding to a full hearing. The respondent should agree an Undertaking only in circumstances when the respondent admits behaviour that might otherwise merit a court order being made against him/her.

The major difference between an Undertaking and a Court Order lies in enforcement of breach:

a) In the case of a breach of a Non-molestation Undertaking, it gives rise to Contempt of Court Enforcement Proceedings, whereas with a breach of a Non-molestation Court Order it is a criminal offence, and if proved will result in a criminal penalty and criminal record.

b) An Occupation Order can have attached to it a power of arrest, so a party breaching it can be arrested and brought to court in custody.

An Occupation Undertaking cannot have a power of arrest attached so the applicant will have to apply to court for a warrant for the respondent's committal.

The advantage of an Undertaking is that an Undertaking is not a Court Order. An Undertaking avoids the risk of criminal penalty for breach, the need for a contested injunction hearing is avoided, and neither party has to give evidence at a trial.

Advocates at these hearings should ensure that their client's case is put to the court at each stage of the proceedings including the court hearings. Negotiations and discussions frequently take place between the parties at the adjourned hearing in order to arrive at an agreement for the making of an order and the terms of such an order. Discussions on the possibility of an Undertaking can take place. In the event of a dispute, the court will be asked to adjudicate on the issues, following representations by all the party's advocates. Parties may be expected to give evidence.

Service of Court Orders

The applicant is responsible for serving the court order by handing a copy of the order to the respondent. This should usually be undertaken by a Process Server. The respondent must know there is an injunction in place to be responsible for breaching any part of it. The applicant is only protected once the respondent is aware of the order. A copy of the order should also be delivered to the local police station.

Breach of a Court Order

If the respondent breaches the injunction, the applicant will need to enforce it. If the respondent has breached the Non-molestation Order it can be enforced by either by reporting his behaviour to the police or commencing civil proceedings by applying to the court that made the order for the respondent to be arrested and/or punished.

Breaching a Non-molestation Order is a criminal offence that can be dealt with by the criminal court. The criminal courts have a range of sentencing options available to them. The maximum sentence is 5 years imprisonment and a fine.

If an Occupation Order is in place, the process for enforcing the order varies depending on whether a power of arrest is attached to the order. A power of arrest allows police officers to arrest the respondent if the occupation order is breached. A power of arrest can be attached to an Occupation Order if the court is satisfied that the respondent has used or threatened violence against the applicant. If the abuser breaches any part of the Occupation Order and there is a power of arrest attached to it, the applicant can report the breach directly to the police.

The Police can arrest him/her and bring him before the court that made the order to be punished. The court may hear evidence about the breach and deal with the respondent immediately, or the court may adjourn the hearing to another day.

If an Occupation Order does not have a power of arrest attached, the applicant can still apply to the court that made the order to have the abuser arrested and/or punished, if he/she has breached any part of the Order. A respondent who is found by the court to have breached the order may be committed to prison, fined or be given a suspended sentence of imprisonment.

CHAPTER 18

OTHER FAMILY PROCEEDINGS

Harassment

If the applicant is not 'associated' with the abuser, the applicant may still be able to obtain protection if he/she is suffering harassment or being put in fear of violence. *The Protection from Harassment Act 1997* makes it a criminal offence to harass someone or make them fear violence will be used against them. The applicant can apply for an Injunction against the person harassing him/her or making him/er fear violence and can also claim damages from him/her.

Definition of harassment

Harassment is a course of conduct that is deliberately intended to cause a person distress or alarm. A course of conduct means two or more incidents of harassment. When deciding whether any particular course of conduct amounts to harassment, the court will consider whether a reasonable person would think that it amounts to harassment.

Examples of harassment could be:

- a text, answer-phone message, letter or email
- a comment or threat
- standing outside someone's house or driving past it
- an act of violence.

Putting someone in fear of violence is a course of conduct that causes another person to fear that violence will be used against them. A person is guilty of putting someone in fear of violence if their behaviour is such that a reasonable person, with the same information, should know that the behaviour would cause them to have that fear.

Protection from harassment and being put in fear of violence

The victim can report an incident of harassment or being put in fear of violence to the police. The Police may give the abuser a warning of the consequences of his behaviour or arrest him for the criminal offences of harassment or putting someone in fear of violence.

The criminal courts, can make a Restraining Order if the abuser is found guilty or if he is acquitted of the offence. The Crown Prosecution Service (CPS) can request the Restraining Order which can prohibit an abuser from doing anything specified in the order including using or threatening violence against the victim, communicating by phone or email or going to certain places such as a home or place of work. In addition to or instead of contacting the police, the victim can apply for an injunction under the *Protection From Harassment Act 1997*. The victim can also ask for damages from the abuser.

Cohabitation

The law treats cohabitants on relationship breakdown as two unrelated individuals. No account is taken of their relationship in terms of financial or other contributions they may have made in order to determine a fair outcome between them on separation or death. This is in spite of many couples being in long-term relationships and/or having children together. Cohabitation does not provide an automatic or guaranteed right to ownership of a partner's property. Cohabitants can apply under *Section 14 of the Trusts of Land and Trustees Act 1996* for the court to determine whether or not a party has an interest in a property, the extent of such interest and how that interest is to be realised. The court has no power to override the strict legal ownership of property and divide it as it may do on divorce or dissolution of a civil partnership. Cohabitation disputes can only be determined where rules of Trusts or Proprietary Estoppel apply. In some circumstances, a former cohabitant may apply for an order for financial provision in the form of transfer or settlement of property orders, periodical payments or lump sum orders on behalf of their children under *Schedule 1 Children Act 1989*. However, this only provides short term relief as orders only continue until a child reaches the age of 18 or ceases full time education.

The surviving cohabitant of a partner who dies without leaving a will, has no automatic right under the intestacy rules to inherit any part of his/her partner's estate. A surviving cohabitant may be able to make a claim under the *Inheritance (Provision for Family and Dependants) Act* 1975 if no provision or inadequate provision has been made for them either by will or by operation of the intestacy rules, but cohabitants are not treated in the same way as a spouse.

Schedule 1 Children Act 1989

In some circumstances where a couple have children, whether or not they ever lived together, there is an option for making an application to the court for an order under *Schedule 1 Children Act 1989* for the following:-

1. Maintenance to be paid for a child if one parent lives abroad, or where the non-resident parent earns more than the maximum amount the CSA or CMS will take into account. The latter are known as "Top Up" orders. The court may also make maintenance orders to pay for educational expenses, a child's disability, or where a child is over the age of 18 and is remaining in education. A child going to University may make an application him/herself.

2. Capital orders. A lump sum or sums may be ordered to be paid nominally for a particular expense e.g. to pay for a family car. There is no limit on the number of lump sum applications that can be made.

3. A property to be transferred or held in trust for the benefit of a child temporarily usually until a child attains the age of 18 or ceases full time secondary or university education. At that stage, the property will either be returned to the payer or sold and the proceeds returned to the payer.

Forced Marriages

A number of designated courts have powers to prevent forced marriages, and to offer protection to victims who might have already been forced into a marriage.

PART C

COURT

CHAPTER 19

ARRIVING AT COURT

Security Check

For those attending a court hearing, bags and pockets will be checked like they would be at an airport. This may include: emptying pockets into a tray, taking off shoes, coat, gloves, hat or belt and walking through an archway detector or being checked with a handheld scanner. Security staff will keep any items not taken into the building and will be give a receipt. In some courts, advocates in possession of a permit may be entitled to fact track the queue.

Court Lists

In most courts there is a list of cases on the wall near the entrance or reception desk. This list usually shows where the case is to be heard, giving the court number, the time of the hearing and the name of the Judge who will deal with the case. The purpose of the list is to enable parties and their advocates to identify easily when and where the case is to be heard. In family cases, the names of the parties are not always listed but the case is identified by the case number set out in the court documents.

Usher

Court Ushers are Court employees who make sure that everyone involved with a court case is present and that they know what to do. Their day-to-day responsibilities include: ensuring that the courtroom is prepared for the hearing, greeting those coming to court for hearings, calling witnesses and parties into court and directing witnesses in the taking of oaths. An usher is often identified by the wearing of a court gown and carrying a clip board with a court list attached.

Waiting areas

Public waiting areas are usually accessible from the main public entrances. Seating areas are also provided. Public toilets, pay telephones, and water fountains are often located near these areas. Waiting space varies according to the court in question. A public address system facilitates moving people from the waiting area to the court rooms at the appropriate times.

Interview rooms

Whilst most courts have private interview rooms for advocates to meet with their clients, there is often a limited number available and means advocates have to see their clients elsewhere in the court building.

Court Clerk

The Court Clerk is a court employee and sits in front of the Judge's bench. He/she helps the Judge make sure the case runs smoothly. They keep a record of the hearing including a note of people attending.

Legal Advisor

A Legal Advisor is a legally qualified person who helps Lay Magistrates apply the law and procedure in the Family Court. They do not play any part in the decision making process, but are there to advise the Court on points of law and procedure. In addition, Legal Advisers are able to carry out the 'gate keeper' function to determine which court will hear a case. The Legal Advisor can make certain procedural orders which are uncontroversial or agreed, as well as sit to hear first hearings in private children cases.

CHAPTER 20

INSIDE THE COURT ROOM

Bowing in Court

As persons enter the court room, whether Court officials, lawyers or members of the public, it is customary to bow to the Royal Coat of Arms and indirectly those presiding over the case. This is in recognition of the fact that justice stems from the Monarch and that Law Courts are part of the Royal Court. Those present in Court should stand up from their seat when the Judge or Lay Magistrate enters the room, "all rise" will be declared, to show respect for them as representatives of the Crown.

Those who can come into the Court Room

The general rule is that Family cases are heard in private. The exceptions are: divorce hearings; contempt of court applications; committal order applications.

In certain types of cases the Court has the power to direct that the case be heard in open Court, for example, non-molestation applications.

The general public are not allowed in Court. Family members or friends are not usually permitted into the court room. Children are usually left outside the court room.

The only people normally allowed in Court are:

- The parties in the Court Proceedings being heard;

- The lawyers for the parties;

- The Judge and the Court staff

- Cafcass officers or Local Authority social workers;

- Witnesses, whilst they are giving evidence;

- The media, although the Court can exclude their attendance in certain cases;

- An Interpreter

- A McKenzie Friend with the permission of the Court;

- Anyone else with the permission of the Court eg a supporter for one of the parties who is vulnerable.

Recordings of the Court Hearing

All court proceedings are audio recorded. The making of a recording is now a part of the **Family Procedure Rules rule 27.9** which requires a recording to be made of a hearing. Most courts now record digitally with court staff logging and downloading the day's audio recordings onto dvd at the end of the court day. This recording will be made of the whole hearing, including any part where the Judge gives a judgment.

Other than pressing stop and start, Judges have no involvement with the process of recording and storage of the official recordings. When a transcript request is made this is dealt with by court staff. It will be court staff who will locate the disc and convey it to the transcription company.

The parties to a case don't have the general right to listen to or obtain a copy of the actual recording of a hearing and they are prohibited from making their own unless the Judge gives permission **s9 Contempt of**

Court Act 1981. A party can ask for permission to obtain a transcript of the recording on payment of a fee.

Interpreters

The Family Court will, if necessary, provide an interpreter if the case involves children, domestic violence or forced marriage. A party might still be able to have an interpreter if he/she can't afford to pay for an interpreter, don't qualify for legal aid and don't have a friend or family member who the Judge says can act as your interpreter. If a party is deaf or hard of hearing, an interpreter will be made available.

Video Link evidence

A video link in court allows a witness to give evidence from a remote location via video. They will appear on-screen in the courtroom and a camera in the Court will allow them to also monitor the proceedings. Arrangements will be made by the court staff following a direction of the Court.

Electronic devices

Before entering court all electronic devices must be turned off. It is a criminal offence to use mobile phones or undertake any recording of Proceedings.

CHAPTER 21

DIFFERENT TRIBUNALS

LAY MAGISTRATES WITH LEGAL ADVISOR

General

Usually three magistrates sit. They are not legally qualified but undertake some training to carry out their role. There will be a chairperson and two magistrates 'on the wings'. The hearing is in private and the court papers are confidential. A court usher will be present in court who often wears a court black gown and carries a clip board with the list of cases attached to it. A legal advisor will also be present in court to assist the magistrates and advise on the law and procedure. He/she is likely to be a qualified Solicitor and employed by HM Court Service.

Advocates address the chairperson not the legal advisor, even though the legal advisor is often involved in directing the proceedings. Advocates will usually be seated on the front bench of the court during the hearing unless the court directs otherwise. The parties will sit close to their Solicitor immediately behind him/her or at their side. Only advocates are expected to address the court. The exception will be when a party is not legally represented. In this case, the unrepresented party (known as a Litigant in Person) will sit on the front bench and address the court personally.

Advocates will address the chairperson as "Sir" or "Madam"

The legal advisor will call the case, briefly explain the nature of the application and then ask the advocate for the applicant to take matters forward. The applicant's advocate will introduce the parties and explain the reason for the hearing.

Types of Application

Most private children cases can be heard by Lay magistrates. These include Section 8 applications: Child Arrangements Orders, Specific Issue Orders, Prohibitive Steps Orders. In addition Special Guardianship and Adoption Orders are heard as well as applications for Non-molestation and Occupation orders. Public Law Orders including Care and Supervision Orders are frequently heard by Lay magistrates. In practice, many of the uncomplicated children cases are heard by Lay magistrates, as are non-molestation and occupation orders. An application can be transferred to another court at any stage in the proceedings.

The Hearing

The advocate for the applicant will present the case on behalf of his/her client by introducing the case, with reference to the court bundle. Depending on the purpose of the hearing, the respondent will be asked to reply to the application by setting out the respondent's case.

If the Lay magistrates are being asked to decide on a particular issue immediately they will usually retire to the their room to discuss matters and then return to court to announce their decision, giving reasons for making such an order. The court will often draft the court order and hand a copy to the parties before they leave the court. If the court hears evidence on oath, a tape recording will be made of that evidence.

DISTRICT JUDGE

General

A District Judge will hear cases that are often too complicated for the Lay Magistrates to deal with. The style of the hearing can be quite different to a hearing before Lay Magistrates. The District Judge is a qualified Solicitor or Barrister and is employed by the HM Court Service to hear family law cases. He/she will have practiced family law for many years prior to being appointed to the court bench. He/she sits alone and will tend to take a proactive role in any hearing. The District Judge will be addressed as Judge. If a decision is required about an issue in the proceedings, the district Judge will usually decide on this matter there and then and give reasons for doing so. The advocate will often be asked to draft the court order and submit this document to the court by email for approval by the District Judge. Hearings are conducted with all parties seated. The formation of the court furniture can vary from court to court. The parties will sit alongside their advocate during the hearing. All hearings are tape recorded.

Types of Applications

A District Judge will hear cases that are often complex in law or procedure. Urgency may be a further reason for a District Judge hearing a case. It could be that there is a discreet issue within the proceedings beyond the experience of Lay magistrates. The District Judge can make a decision on that matter and then transfer to the Lay Magistrates to hear the remaining part of the case. In addition to all matters heard by Lay Magistrates, a District Judge can hear court applications that flow from divorce proceedings including financial and property applications as well as claims by cohabitants. Other applications relating financial provision for children are within the remit of a District Judge.

CIRCUIT JUDGE

General

A Circuit Judge is the more senior judge in a court circuit. Some have the title 'Designated Family Judge' who undertake a supervisory role in overseeing the judicial work in a court area. The Circuit Judge is addressed as 'Your Honour.' An advocate sits on the front bench of the court room, will stand to address the Judge but will remain seated during the other parts of the hearing. The parties will sit on the bench immediately behind their advocate.

Types of Application

Whilst a Circuit Judge is able to hear any case more usually heard by Lay Magistrates or a District Judge, he/she will focus on more complex, long and urgent family proceedings. Commonly, a Circuit Judge will handle complex care proceedings.

CHAPTER 22

TYPES OF HEARINGS

Without Notice Hearings

In certain circumstances, an application can be made for the court to hear an application without the other party knowing about it. At a Without Notice Hearing, the applicant must show that the making of the order is urgent. One example might be taking a child abroad before the hearing as it would not be safe if the applicant gave notice to the other party. A further example may be if an applicant has been threatened with abuse. During a Without Notice Hearing, the Judge will hear the applicant's reasons for making the application without informing the other party. The court may make the order requested or may postpone making the order until it has heard from the other party. Even if the court makes the order requested, it will usually set a date for a further hearing to decide whether or not the order should continue. The other party will be informed of this hearing date and asked to attend a further hearing to put forward their views. The Without Notice Hearing is likely to take a more informal approach with the Judge reading the papers and making a decision often without hearing any formal evidence.

Directions Hearings

A Directions Hearing is listed for the Judge to review the case and consider whether further information should be provided or action taken by the parties within the proceedings such as Cafcass or any other relevant body. Advocates representing the parties will usually meet together before the hearing to agree the terms of the court order and prepare a draft of the order. The Court will consider the draft order and make any appropriate amendments. In the event of a disagreement between the parties, the Judge will adjudicate on the matter. Representations by the advocates will usually be in the form of submissions, quite often by consenting to the terms of the agreed order. No evidence is heard. Judges and Lay Magistrates are encouraged to manage cases to ensure that the proceedings are progressed in the appropriate way.

Case Management Hearings

- Case management takes place when decisions are made by the court on such matters as:

- the key issues to be determined

- whether the proceedings should be listed for a fact-finding hearing,

- whether any interim orders need to made pending a final hearing,

- whether directions are required to ensure the final hearing proceeds as planned.

The hearing takes a similar form to that of directions but is more structured and focused in content. Case management is common in Care and Supervision Proceedings.

Contested Interim Hearings

Interim Orders can be made by the court until final orders are made. The hearing often takes the form of a full hearing when evidence is heard by the court and a decision is made pending the final decision of the Court. Examples are: Interim Care or Supervision Orders and Interim Child Arrangements Orders.

Fact Finding Hearings

If one party makes allegations during family law proceedings and the other party denies those allegations, the Judge will consider whether there should be a Fact Finding Hearing. This is a separate hearing arranged to decide whether or not the allegations are true. Fact Finding Hearings are most common in children cases, but can also take place during other family law proceedings such as for domestic abuse injunctions, or financial remedies.

Final Hearings

The final hearing brings the proceedings to an end. The Judge or Lay Magistrates will consider all of the available evidence. This includes evidence provided by the parties and any relevant reports provided by others such as Cafcass or the Local Authority. Using all of this information, the Judge will assess the evidence and come to a decision. The Judge may decide to make no order or make an order requested by the parties. The format of the final hearing can take various forms: An Agreed Order, a Contested Hearing (when evidence is heard) or a hearing where the parties make oral submissions without any evidence being called. This depends on the nature of the final hearing.

CHAPTER 23

EVIDENCE ON OATH

A witness will be shown to the witness box by the court usher. The witness should stand up to take the oath, but if he/she finds standing difficult, they can ask the Lay Magistrate or the Judge if you can sit down. They will be asked to take the oath. Sworn testimony is evidence given by a witness who has made a commitment to tell the truth. If the witness is later found to have lied whilst bound by the commitment, they can be charged with the crime of perjury.

The types of commitment can include oaths, affirmations and promises.

The commitment can come in different forms depending on the situation of the witness.

These are:

- **Oath**: A commitment made to the witness's deity, or on their holy book

- **Affirmation**: A secular variant of the oath where the witness does not have to mention a deity or holy book

- **Promise**: A commitment made by a witness under the age of 17, or of all witnesses if none of the accused are over the age of 17.

In England and Wales the wording is:

Oath:

I swear by [substitute Almighty God/Name of God (such as Jehovah) or the name of the holy scripture] the evidence I shall give shall be the truth, the whole truth, and nothing but the truth.

Affirmation:

I do solemnly and sincerely and truly declare and affirm that the evidence I shall give shall be the truth, the whole truth, and nothing but the truth.

Promise:

I promise before Almighty God that the evidence which I shall give shall be the truth, the whole truth, and nothing but the truth.

In the UK, a person may give testimony at any age, but will not be sworn in unless 14 years old or over.

CHAPTER 24

REMOTE COURT HEARINGS IN FAMILY PROCEEDINGS

Remote hearings

A remote hearing is one which is held without the people involved attending court in person. Instead they join the hearing by telephone or by video link using their phone or another device such as laptop or tablet. Sometimes the judge will be at home rather than in the court building. Apart from the fact that people are not in the same building, a remote hearing is exactly the same as a hearing where the parties attend to court in person and the process is broadly the same. The court has all the same powers and will expect people to treat it just as seriously as a 'normal' hearing.

Hybrid hearings

A hybrid hearing is a mixture of a remote hearing and a 'normal' hearing. This means that some of the people involved attend the court in person, and some of them join the hearing remotely by video link or phone. A hybrid hearing might happen if one person cannot physically travel to court. This can happen in some family cases where there are several parties involved. In some cases, one party might attend the courtroom (or another building) so they can be in the same room as their solicitor, but still join the actual hearing by video link. There are a number of different combinations depending on the type of case and the particular circumstances.

The remote hearing itself

When court hearings take place in person in a court building, they do not always start on time because judges often allow parties and their lawyers some flexibility to have discussions before going into the courtroom. It could also be that there are several cases listed at the same time. Remote hearings almost always start on time. It is important that any discussions between the parties have taken place before the start time for the hearing, and that they are ready and waiting at the time the hearing is listed.

It often takes a few minutes for everyone to join the hearing.

At the start of the hearing the Judge will explain that the hearing is being recorded and that It is a criminal offence to record the hearing without permission. If the hearing is heard in private, which is the case for most family court hearings, the Judge will check with everyone involved in the case that they are on their own and somewhere private.

The Judge will make sure people take turns in speaking, and will ask those present not to interrupt. It is a good policy for everyone to put themselves on 'mute' except when they are actually talking, so that background noise does not stop people hearing what is being said. The parties should make sure that, if possible, they have the bundle or the most important documents accessible for reference purposes. Judges can and do hear evidence from witnesses at remote hearings, and can make final orders. It will be for the Judge to decide whether it is fair and suitable for a particular hearing to be dealt with remotely and, if not, what the alternative arrangements can be made.

Joining a remote hearing

The parties will be sent joining instructions before the hearing, either by the court or by the solicitor who is organising the connection.

If the hearing is a telephone hearing, this will usually be arranged by the court and they will call the parties so they can take part. It is important to make sure the court has your up-to-date phone number and that the parties are ready to answer the call when it comes in. The parties should ensure their phone or device is charged or connected to power so that it does not run out of battery during the hearing. If the court is unable to reconnect to a party during the hearing, it might continue on without them. If the hearing is a video hearing, it could be run through one of several different platforms.

Devices, apps or software

The basic requirement is a functioning phone with a reliable connection. Even if the hearing is a video hearing, a party can still join by phone, but it is much easier to follow by video. There are a number of different video platforms that can be used to run a remote hearing, but most of them work in a very similar way. With some video platforms, you might be invited to download an app, but if you prefer, most platforms allow you to join through your internet browser. Cloud Video Platform (CVP) is the Court Service's own video platform. It works through a browser and can be used without needing to download an app.

Support during the remote hearings

If a hearing is a family case the parties should be on your own unless the Judge gives you permission for someone else to be with them. A supporter could be a carer, an Independent Domestic Violence Advocate, a social worker or other support / key worker, a family member or friend or a 'McKenzie Friend'. A supporter might be in the same location as a party during the hearing or they might join the hearing from somewhere else. If the hearing is in private, the Judge may ask the supporter to confirm they understand that they must keep things private, before the hearing goes ahead. Anyone who does attend a hearing to support a party they should remain silent throughout.

If possible, any children should be safely occupied, out of earshot and supervised in another room during the hearing. This is particularly important if it is a family matter about them. A party can still ask the judge about a supporter at the start of the hearing if they have not been able to do this in advance of the hearing.

Communications during the hearing

If a party has a solicitor or supporter, discussions about the best way of communicating during a remote hearing should take in advance of the hearing. Normally a party could whisper to their solicitor in the courtroom, but in a remote hearing they could use WhatsApp, or email, or a separate video link or phone call to communicate privately as things happen. On some platforms, it is possible to set up a private 'room 'where a party can have private discussions with their solicitor or supporter (a breakout room).

Requests for a face-to-face hearing

If a party considers there is a need for a face-to-face court hearing this should be raised with the court. The judge has to make a decision on a case-by-case basis depending on:

- the nature of the case and the specific hearing

- the particular needs of the people involved

- what is safe and practical.

If a party has a disability that makes a remote hearing impractical or unsuitable, or if there is a need for an adjustment to be made so that a party can participate the party concerned should raise the matter with the court.

Difficulties during the hearing

It is important that the parties understand what is happening during the hearing. If a party is struggling to see, hear or follow, they should let the judge know at the time. They can do this by speaking, putting their hand up or (on some platforms) pressing a button to raise a 'virtual 'hand. The judge may ask everyone who is not speaking to mute their microphones. Sometimes people get cut off from a hearing part way through. Usually the people left behind will get a notification telling them a party has gone, so they will either try and rejoin. If the internet connection goes down, it might be possible to join by telephone.

The Court Order

The court will produce an order recording the outcome of the hearing, and will send everyone involved a copy of the order. If there are lawyers involved they will prepare the order for the judge, and the solicitor will send out the order once it has been approved.

Further Information

The Courts and Tribunals Service (HMCTS) have produced a Guide on Joining Court Hearings by Video Call or Phone:

https://assets.publishing.service.gov.uk/government/uploads/system/uploads/attachment_data/file/876566/

HMCTS have also produced a Guide to How to join Cloud Video Platform (CVP) for a video hearing:

https://www.gov.uk/government/publications/how-to-join-a-cloud-video-platform-cvp-hearing/how-to-join-cloud-video-platform-cvp-for-a-video-hearing

PART D

PROCEDURES

CHAPTER 25

ALTERNATIVES TO COURT PROCEEDINGS

Mediation

Mediation is a form of negotiation facilitated by a neutral third party within a structured process. The parties agree to the appointment of an impartial third person to assist them to communicate better with one another and reach their own agreed and informed decisions concerning some, or all, of the issues relating to separation, divorce, children, finance or property by negotiation.

- Mediators are independent and impartial, qualified professionals with a range of backgrounds from law to healthcare. They work to facilitate a settlement which is tailored to the parties' needs and interests rather than imposing or deciding the final outcome. Mediators can assist with communication and help reduce conflict and dispute going forward. Their role is to organise the process, facilitate the process and act as an intermediary between the parties.

- Mediation can take place at any stage of the dispute but it is most effective at an early stage. The President of the Family Division is keen to promote mediation and it is an important plank of the 'Supporting Separating Family Alliance' proposed by the second report of the Working Group on Private Law Cases chaired by Cobb J (12 March 2020).

- A mediation agreement should be entered into at the start. The agreement will include practical matters, mediator's fees, confidentiality clause, immunity clause etc. Typically mediation goes through four stages:

1. opening: open meeting where there is an introduction, parties' opening positions and mediator's remarks;

2. exploration: through a combination of open and closed meetings where the mediator explores the issues and strategies for settlement;

3. negotiation: mostly through closed meetings the mediator acts as a broker between parties who consider and make offers, and helps parties work through deadlock;

4. closing: open meeting to confirm terms of settlement or summarise the closing positions if settlement is not reached.

- If an agreement is reached, the mediator will draw up a Memorandum of Understanding. This can then be made legally binding by the court in the form of a consent order.

www.lawsociety.org.uk/support-services/advice/articles/consent-order-guidance/

- **Mediation Vouchers**

On 26 March 2021, the Ministry of Justice launched a mediation voucher scheme which will contribute up to £500 towards mediation costs in eligible cases. On attendance at a MIAM, the mediator will assess whether a party meets the eligibility requirements. The case types for which a voucher may be claimed are a dispute/application relating to a child or a dispute/application regarding family financial matters which also involves a dispute/application relating to a child. **Practice Direction 36V – Pilot Scheme: Family Mediation Voucher Scheme, published on 26 March 2021.**

www.familymediationcouncil.org.uk/mediation-voucher-scheme

- **Mediation must be attempted in earnest**

A Judge may to refuse to hear a case where mediation has not been attempted. The Judge may adjourn a case, at any stage, for mediation to be attempted. Parties are expected, now more than ever, to try mediation earnestly (*Re B (a child) (Unnecessary Private Law Applications) [2020]*). The Judge warned parties and lawyers against making unnecessary applications. Part of a solicitor's role is to persuade clients that going to court really is a last resort.

- **Mediation Information and Assessment Meetings (MIAMs)**

s10(1) Children and Families Act 2014 provides that: *Before making a relevant family application, a person must attend a family mediation information and assessment meeting.* This means that MIAMs are compulsory and so all clients will be expected to attend such a meeting before making an application to the court. A *relevant family application* is defined by **s10(3)** as an application which (a) is made to the court in, or to initiate, family proceedings and (b) is of a description specified in **FPR**. This will include all the most usual applications in private law proceedings relating to children and in proceedings for a financial remedy.

> (a) A MIAM is a meeting with a specially qualified family mediator, who can explain the alternatives to the court process. Divorcing and separating couples who want to use the court process to resolve any questions about children or money have to show that they have attended a MIAM before they can apply for a court order. Most applications to the Single Family Court require the **Form FM1** confirming mediation has been attempted before they will issue proceedings or a Judge may adjourn a case for the parties to attempt mediation before he will allow the case to proceed.

(b) At a MIAM a qualified family mediator will discuss the client's situation on a confidential basis. If a client is unsure of the process, they may wish to book an individual mediation session to examine how they feel about the process. Usually this is a one-to-one meeting, although sometimes parties attend together if they wish. Currently, only one of the parties is required to attend a MIAM to talk through the alternatives to court and decide whether another route could be appropriate.

(c) If the client has a low income and relatively low capital, they may be entitled to legal aid although not all mediators will conduct legal aid matters.

https://thefma.co.uk/   https://www.familymediationcouncil.org.uk

- **Exemptions to mediation**

A party will not be expected to attend a MIAM if any of the following apply to the situation:

- A party has made an allegation of domestic violence against the other supported by clear evidence.

- An application to the court needs to be made urgently because there is a risk to the life or safety of the person who is making the application.

- The dispute is about money and either party is bankrupt.

- Social Services are involved because there are concerns about the safety and wellbeing of a child.

- In the past four months mediation has been unsuccessfully attempted.

- A mediator signs **Form FM1** confirming that mediation is not suitable, this form must be sent to the court when issuing most family law applications

(https://www.gov.uk/government/publications/give-information-for-a-family-mediation-assessment-form-fm1).

Collaborative law

- Collaborative law is a process in which lawyers and clients work together to resolve a dispute. It aims to address all legal, financial and practical aspects of separation and the parties' future relationship.

- It is most suitable where parties are focused on their children's best interests and/or maintaining or developing a good relationship, and are seeking a solution outside the court process. There must be a constructive and respectful approach with both parties willing to give full disclosure.

- When the collaborative process ends the lawyers can no longer act for the parties.

- The process can be broken down into four stages:

    1. preparation meetings, include: — between each solicitor and client for the solicitor to explain the process, and discuss goals and objectives, and — between the solicitor separately to plan the first meeting;

    2. initial four-way meeting is between all solicitors and clients where the parties seek to lay the foundations and share their objectives. An agenda will be set for the next meeting. Solicitors and clients will sign a four-way agreement committing to work out a settlement without going to court;

135

3. intermediate four-way meetings may be held before all issues are resolved. Each meeting will have an agenda, review progress and revise key issues. Part of their function is for information sharing and gathering. There may be involvement of other professionals such as accountants, pension experts, independent social workers. The lawyers will assist the clients in exploring their options and devising solutions;

4. final four-way meeting happens when an agreement is reached. It will deal with formalities of signing documents. Clients can withdraw from the process at any time but there is usually a cooling off period before proceedings can be initiated. The negotiations cannot be then referred to in evidence.

www.resolution.org.uk/collaborative_process/

Arbitration

- Arbitration offers the opportunity for parties to agree to appoint an independent, qualified professional to adjudicate their dispute and make a binding decision.

- The same arbitrator can deal with all stages of the case from start to finish. This continuity provides reassurance for the parties that the person making the decisions in their case has a real understanding of their situation. Additionally, the parties can have much greater input into how the proceedings are run. This can include whether to meet face to face or in writing only. One benefit is that the parties can use the arbitrator for the whole process. This can also save great expense.

- Arbitration is often quicker and cheaper than the court process. It offers flexibility and privacy. The unique factor is that arbitration offers finality, although in **Haley v Haley [2020] EWCA Civ 1369** the Court of Appeal clarified the route whereby an aggrieved party may challenge an arbitral award and the judgment confirms that the court retains a supervisory jurisdiction under the Matrimonial Causes Act 1973.

The court suggested the primary means for challenging an arbitral award should be under the Arbitration Act 1996.

ifla.org.uk/cms/wp-content/uploads/2015/09/Public.pdf

www.familylawweek.co.uk/site.aspx?i=ed126784

CHAPTER 26

DRAFTING APPLICATIONS AND STATEMENTS

Introduction

A paper application in family court proceedings sets the scene for any family court case. The purpose of the application is not only to tell the court what order you are seeking but to tell others too. There will always be at least one respondent (the applicant's opponent) who needs to know what order the applicant is seeking and the reason why it is filed with the court. It is a principal of natural justice that any respondent has an opportunity to oppose the application and put forward their own case. Court procedure allows any respondent to put their case (usually in writing) and give evidence at a court hearing if necessary.

Applications

1. If your client is seeking an order from the family court you will need to complete an application form and file this with the court together with any other relevant papers.

2. The form itself will depend what order is being sought. If the applicant is seeking a care order or supervision order the form is likely to be **Form C110A**. In the case of a private law application **Form C100**. For a non-molestation order it will be **Form FL401** and for a financial order following divorce it be **Form A**. The form will trigger the beginning of court proceedings. Using the correct form is vital. Otherwise, the application will be delayed or even rejected by the court. So take great care should be taken in choosing the form.

3. The content and the drafting of this form is also very important. It is an opportunity to set out the applicant's case at an early stage.

4. The form will be filed and seen by the court, by the opposing party and in the case of private children proceedings, a copy is also sent to Cafcass.

5. It is not usually possible to file a detailed statement at this point but the form can be used to good effect. If the applicant chooses to use additional pages this is acceptable. The contents of the application form will be read very early in the process and setting out your case at the beginning can be useful. Amending the form at a later stage can be complicated so it is important that the details are accurate and clear.

6. Once the application form is filed with the Family Court the papers will be considered by a court official known as a 'Gatekeeper'.

7. **The Gatekeeper**

    The Gatekeeper (a District Judge or Legal Advisor) will decide on whether the application filed by the applicant is suitable to be heard by the Lay magistrates. In practice, many of the uncomplicated children cases are heard by Lay magistrates, as are non-molestation and occupation orders. Otherwise, the application will be listed before a District Judge or a Circuit Judge. An application can be transferred to another court at any stage in the proceedings if deemed necessary.

8. **Statements**

    In family court proceedings, a witness statement will stand as the party's main evidence to the Judge. The other parent will read the statement before the hearing. Cross examination will be based on what is written in the statement so it is important the contents are accurate. Statements are common in some proceedings and less common in others. For example, statements are usual in care proceedings, injunction cases and some private children applications. They are less common in financial applications.

9. Who makes and files a statement?

- A party to proceedings

- Witnesses including experts

10. General Guidance

The Rules as to the making and filing of statements are set out in **Part 22 FPR 2010** and **Practice Direction 22A**: as to content and style.

https://www.justice.gov.uk/courts/procedure-rules/family/parts/part_22

The President of the Family Division, Sir Andrew McFarlane, has issued a memorandum setting out how witness statements should be prepared for use in the Family Courts to ensure they meet proper professional standards. The full details can be found below.

https://www.judiciary.uk/wp-content/uploads/2021/11/PFD-memo-on-witness-statements-12112021.pdf

- A witness statement should be factual and state what was seen, heard, or felt by the person writing the statement

- A party can only file a statement if the court directs this

- A statement is the main way of setting out a party's case

- Once evidence has been filed no further evidence/statement is permitted without permission of the court

- Statements can be contemporaneous (parties file at the same time) or consecutive (where one party files first and the other files by way of reply)

- A party may, with the court's permission, file witness statements to support their case

- The court can limit the length and content of the statement

- A party can attach exhibits to their statement to great effect: copies of documents including emails, copies of text messages, photographs, video recordings and audio recordings.

- Recent guidance given by the President of Family Division: **Presidents Memorandum: Witness Statements 10th November 2021**

- A party is required to file their statement with the court and serve a copy on the opposing party, and others if appropriate, eg Cafcass, Local Authority or experts

- A party usually files a narrative statement. A position statement can be filed at a later stage often prepared to inform the court of a party's case shortly before a court hearing

- A client should be given a copy of the statement to refresh memory in advance of a court hearing

- Affidavits are sworn statements. They are used infrequently and often when the court feels the need to impress on a party or witness the importance of making a statement that is accurate.

11. How to prepare a statement

- The witness statement must be expressed in the first person using the witness's own words

- If a party's address is confidential it can state that only the court knows the address

- Allow the client to have time to consider before signing the statement. It sets out their evidence to the court so the client needs to be fully in agreement with the contents

- Initially map out the points the statement needs to cover and then expand on the important subjects

- The use of headings can be helpful and makes the reading of the statement easier to follow

- It should be brief, without repetition and relevant

- How much is too much? This is a matter of professional judgment but you should lean on the side of brevity. Resist pressure from the client to unduly attack or criticise the other party, especially in children cases

- At the end of the document set out a 'statement of truth' as to the contents

- Ensure the statement is filed with the court on time, otherwise the court's permission will be required to file it late

- **Templates** are readily available to the parties. They can be used instead of starting a statement with a blank piece of paper. They are often used by a litigant in person and encouraged in their use by the President of the Family Division. They are available from the court office and downloadable on the internet.

https://www.gov.uk/government/publications/form-c120-witness-statement-template-child-arrangements-parental-dispute

https://www.judiciary.uk/wp-content/uploads/2021/11/PFD-memo-on-witness-statements-12112021.pdf

CHAPTER 27

PREPARING OF COURT BUNDLES

The court bundle forms the basis of the court evidence and the means by which the court and all the parties are informed as to what the case is all about. At the court hearing itself, the applicant will present the case often referring to the contents of the bundle. Whilst in the witness box, the witnesses will be asked to look at the court bundle, will be cross examined, usually on the information set out in the bundle. The court is likely to give its decision by reference to the bundle. Consequently, the bundle is a vital part of the court process.

The court bundle

- A bundle is a folder of court documents provided to the court before a hearing and should contain all of the documents the court will need for that hearing.

- The size of the bundle may be different for each hearing, but if the applicant is updating a previous bundle, it is important to keep the same page numbers for the documents already in the bundle.

- In family cases, the court expects a bundle to be prepared for every hearing in the Family court or in the High court. Courts sometimes have their own local practice and which can deviate from the general rules to some extent. If in doubt, follow the local practice.

- Whether you have to prepare the bundle will depend on your position in the case. Normally the solicitor for the applicant prepares the bundle. If there are cross-applications, the solicitor for the party who has made their application first, prepares the bundle. If the applicant is not legally represented, the solicitor for the respondent prepares the bundle. If no one in the case has a solicitor, the court will usually prepare a court bundle.

How it works in practice

- Shortly before a court hearing, a bundle of documents, most of which are in the court file, is delivered the court, usually by the applicant. This may be a paper bundle but possibly an e-bundle. A copy of the bundle is also sent to the respondent and any other parties in the proceedings. Within that bundle will be the statements filed by the parties, as well as other papers that the court will consider as part of the case.

- The size of the bundle will build up the more times the case comes before the court. The bundle commonly starts with just a few papers and by the time the case comes before the court for a full hearing, the bundle has often grown to a couple of hundred pages or more. The size of the bundle often depends the type of application before the court. For example, there will be larger court bundles in financial applications and care proceedings, and smaller bundles in injunction cases and some private children applications.

- At the court hearing itself the applicant will present the case, often referring to the contents of the bundle. The applicant will begin by asking the court if it has received the court bundle and whether it has had an opportunity of reading the contents. The applicant will introduce the case by referring to the contents of the bundle, for example the case summary. If the hearing is a final hearing, the parties may give evidence. The applicant will be called to give evidence on oath. Whilst in the witness box, the applicant will be asked to look at the court bundle, already placed in the witness box. The applicant will be referred to his/her statement (usually by page numbers) and asked to confirm that the contents are true. The applicant may also be referred to other documents in the bundle, as these will form his/her evidence in chief. Unless the statement needs updating, the court will not normally allow any further evidence in chief. The applicant will be cross examined by the respondent on what is said in his/her statement. The same exercise is repeated for the respondent and any witnesses including expert witnesses.

- Court bundles ensure that the court and the parties are made aware of the evidence well in advance of the court hearing. No one should be taken by surprise by what is said in court and there is no 'ambushing' of a party by producing new information at the last minute. The court can give permission for fresh information to be presented to the court but only as an exception to the general rule and with good reason. If one party seeks to introduce fresh evidence the opposing party has the right to object, in which case the court will adjudicate on the issue. It is sometimes said: 'If it is not in the court bundle, the court does not need to hear about it.'

Court Rules regarding Bundles

- **Practice Direction 27A** is the authority for preparing court bundles in family cases. This sets out the way a court bundle should be prepared. You may find it helpful to read it in detail.

https://www.justice.gov.uk/downloads/fjr/pd27A.pdf

- In addition, there are two reported cases.

These are:

L (Procedure: Bundles: Translation) [2015] EWFC 15 in which the President of the Family Division expressed his dismay that PD 27A in relation to the preparation of court bundles was frequently ignored by practitioners. He warned that court staff would be instructed to refuse witness bundles unless a Judge had specifically directed that they would be lodged. It was strongly emphasised that **PD27A** required only documents to be included in the bundle which were relevant and would be used ie read or referred to in the proceedings. Documents should be as short and succinct as possible. The endemic failure to comply with **PD27A** must end now. He went on to say that defaulters could expect to be exposed in public condemnation in judgments in which they would be named and they could find themselves subject to financial penalties.

Re X Re and Y (Bundles) [2008] 2 FLR 2053

This was a judgment concerning the sanctions available to the judiciary where bundles are not supplied in accordance with the Practice Direction. This judgment of Munby J arose from his frustrations at being presented with late and inaccurate bundles. He cites two specific examples but says that these are merely two of many. His main complaints were that bundles are regularly late; they are badly indexed; they contain material that should have been weeded out after previous hearings; and do not provide a skeleton argument. Having set out his complaints, he reiterates the sanctions available including costs orders, moving the case to the end of the list, adjourning altogether or naming and shaming offenders.

What documents go into the bundle?

- The bundle will contain the documents that the court needs for each hearing. If you are preparing a bundle for a short directions hearing, the court is unlikely to need supporting evidence such as police records for that hearing. The court needs *one bundle* for the hearing that includes all of the documents from the parties in the case and any other papers prepared by others, for example Cafcass. You should not include documents in the bundle that have not been filed with the court and served on the parties.

CHAPTER 27

- Bundles are always broken up into sections which are divided by file dividers that are given a letter:

    C.   Preliminary documents,

    D.   Applications and Orders,

    E.   Statements and Affidavits,

    F.   Care Plans (where appropriate)

    G.   Experts and other reports,

    H.   Other documents ...

What are Preliminary Documents (Section A) ?

- Preliminary documents are **not** evidence. They are meant to summarise information for the court so that it can understand what the case is about and the purpose of the hearing.

The Preliminary Documents are:

• A case summary

This is a summary of the background to the hearing limited to the issues that are relevant to the hearing. This document should be neutral between the parties.

• A statement of issues

This document should set out the questions the court will be asked to decide at that hearing and at the final hearing.

149

- **A position statement**

This document is individual for each party – it should explain to the court what a party's position is for that hearing.

- **A chronology for a final hearing.**

This is a list of dates, starting with the oldest, when important things happened, for example, the dates of birth of any children, dates of incidents of domestic violence, dates of applications to court and hearings.

- **A skeleton argument**

This is a document summarising the legal points the parties wish to make and how they relate to the case.

- **Time estimate for the hearing.**

This is used at fact finding or final hearings when the court will hear from witnesses. Each witness should be listed with a time estimate for roughly how long it will take the court to hear from them.

- **A list of essential reading for the hearing.**

This is a list of the documents the court should read before that hearing. This can be very useful in cases where there is a large court bundle as the list will highlight the more important documents to consider in advance of the hearing.

Size of the court bundle

- Bundles should not be any larger than 350 pages.

- If a bundle is larger than 350 pages, the applicant should raise this with the court and seek a direction that permission is given for the bundle to be larger than 350 pages.

- Only one bundle needs to be prepared for each hearing. This bundle should be an agreed bundle. This means it will include all of the documents that the parties wish the court to see for that hearing. The party who prepares the bundle (usually the applicant) will put together the documents and prepare a draft index. If you are trying to agree a bundle with the other party, you will need to send them a draft index with enough time to make suggestions for changes. At this stage do not write the numbers on your documents in case you have to change them later. If changes need to be made or documents added or removed, this can be done before the index is finally agreed. Once you have an agreed index, you can number all of the pages.

E Bundles

- Courts have become increasingly accustomed to using e bundles. It does depend on which court hears the case. Some courts are more advanced on this than others

- The Courts and Tribunals Judiciary have issued general guidance on electronic court bundles.

- The guidance is intended to ensure consistency in the provision of electronic bundles for court hearings in a format that promotes the efficient preparation for a hearing.

- The guidance covers such subjects as format, page numbering, indexing and style of presentation and the delivering of e-bundles.

https://www.judiciary.uk/announcements/general-guidance-on-electronic-court-bundles/

https://www.judiciary.uk/wp-content/uploads/2021/12/Sup-guidance-E-bundles.pdf

- Particular help on the use and workings of e-bundles in the family court can be found in a guide prepared by 3PB Barristers. This includes a series of video guides dealing with creating, numbering, updating and sending large files.

www.3pb.co.uk/expertise/family/how-to-create-ebundles-for-the-family-court

Unrepresented litigants

- Ordinarily, the applicant is responsible for preparing the court bundle. If the applicant is an unrepresented litigant and the other party is legally represented, then that party should prepare the bundle. This is often incorporated into the court directions prior to the hearing. If neither party is legally represented, the court will often prepare the bundle.

https://resolution.org.uk/guidance-note-court-bundles/

CHAPTER 28

INSTRUCTING COUNSEL

Introduction

In England and Wales, separate sections of the legal profession exist. Barristers can also be referred to as 'counsel'. They are 'members of the Bar. Barristers are not limited to accepting instructions from law firms. Where a barrister is briefed directly by the client it is referred to as 'Direct Access'.

Reasons for Instructing Counsel

- Counsel can provide expertise which the law firm does not possess. This expertise may relate to a specialised area of family law. The Bar consists of specialist advocates and few solicitors have the opportunity to develop the level of advocacy skills and experience possessed by many barristers. Solicitors often find it advantageous to be able to obtain a second opinion from an independent legal practitioner.

- Barristers can provide a very cost-effective service. Barristers, and especially more junior barristers, can provide their services at a much cheaper daily or hourly rate than solicitors of equivalent standing.

Selecting Counsel appropriate for the task

- Many firms have a set of chambers whom they usually brief. If your firm has a good working relationship with a particular barrister, then it is a very good reason to use this barrister if the matter in question falls within the range of the barrister's experience or expertise.

- When choosing barristers, three factors should be taken into account: seniority, specialisation and experience. Seniority normally carries with it a higher price tag. There are two levels of barristers: junior barristers (who vary in experience from being newly qualified to very experienced practitioners) and KCs (who hold the title for their exceptional ability and competence). Fee structures within the Bar vary ranging from junior barristers who may charge as little as a few hundred pounds per day, up to the top KCs at thousands of pounds per day. It is important to brief a barrister in matters involving an issue of law within the barrister's area of specialisation. In order to choose counsel best qualified for the task in hand, you may need to seek advice from others in your firm, or from lawyers in other firms.

Arrange conferences where necessary or appropriate
A pre-trial conference is where the barrister meets the client, discusses their evidence and offers them advice as to the manner in which they may give their evidence. Such conferences can be very helpful in cases where a client is planning to give oral testimony. It may be that no court proceedings have commenced but the client has asked for advice in anticipation of such proceedings. This can take place remotely by Zoom or Teams usually set up by the instructing Solicitor making the arrangements and for counsel and the client to be invited to attend. This will enable action to be taken on matters advised by counsel.

Counsels' fees

- The situation regarding fees for counsel must be clearly understood by all concerned. Disputes relating to fees are one of the two main sources of disagreement between solicitors and members of the Bar. Such disputes can be minimised by ensuring that the situation is clearly explained and understood.

- If the fee is a fixed one – such as a Legal Aid scale fee – or has been negotiated in advance, this should be clearly confirmed with the brief. You will provide the legal aid certificate number with the papers. The responsibility of paying counsel's fees rests with the instructing solicitor. If you have any doubts about the client's ability to pay, or the client's willingness to pay, you should ensure that you have funds on account before counsel is briefed.

- It is also the responsibility of solicitors to remit funds to counsel as soon as counsel has performed the work.

- From time to time, problems arise in relation to paying counsel's fees, either because the client is not forthcoming with funds, or because funds held from the client prove to be insufficient. In such a case, it remains the professional responsibility of the Solicitor to pay counsel's fees, even if the firm has to pay those fees from its own resources.

Style of Brief or Instructions to Counsel

- Instructions can be to advise in writing, to advise in conference or to attend a court hearing (brief). There is no strict form which this document must take, and its contents will depend on the nature of the particular case. Some practical points:

    - Instructions are usually given in chronological order.

    - It is helpful if the brief is in a ring binder which allows pages to be inserted and removed easily.

    - Separate the divisions in the brief with cardboard 'dividers'

- Original documents such as title deeds, mortgages, signed contracts should not be included in a brief to counsel. There is always a risk that such documents may go astray.

- If there is something that counsel should know about as soon as he or she receives the brief, it should be marked on the outside of the brief, preferably in large red lettering. This is particularly important if there is a time-limit, such as a limitations period due to expire in the near future.

- Identify, on the outside of the brief, hearing dates or dates of other forthcoming court appearances. This enables the barrister, or the barrister's clerk, to ensure that the correct dates are in the barrister's diary and conflicting engagements are avoided.

- It is helpful to identify the individual within the law firm whom the barrister should contact if it is necessary to discuss the matter. This should include the individual's direct telephone number and email address.

- If more than one barrister is briefed in the same case, the brief should also identify, preferably on the outer cover the name of the leader or junior

- Counsel's brief will be updated for each subsequent hearing.

- It is increasingly common for solicitors to brief barristers by email, without providing documents in hard copy.

Content of Brief

- Ensure that the Brief includes everything that Counsel will need. If you are not sure whether or not a particular document is relevant you should include it.

- Include a brief summary of the facts and issues by way of a broad 'over-view' of the case. You should not go into to extensive detail which is set out fully in witness statements and documentary evidence,

- Observations highlighting specific issues potentially problematic should be included which cross-references to witness statements and items of documentary evidence regarded as critically important.

- Instructions are not intended to take the place of proper witness statements. If the Instructing Solicitors are aware of relevant facts which may not emerge from witness statements, it may be convenient to mention these. Except in the very simplest cases, it is unacceptable however merely to summarise the client's instructions without furnishing a proper statement.

- Instructions to advise should also elaborate on precisely what counsel is instructed to do. In the case of a request to provide an opinion, it is often useful for the solicitors to specify precisely the questions and issues which counsel is required to address – advice on evidence, or advice on prospects of success, or advice on some specific legal issue.

Layout of Brief

- Written in third person

- Heading-court proceedings or name of client

- Who you are and for whom you act

- Nature of dispute

- Brief background with relevant events and chronology

- Deadlines-hearing dates-time limits

- Your requirements of the barrister

- Contact details

- Legal Aid reference number

Attendance at court

Traditionally lawyers have accompanied their client in attending court with counsel. The Solicitor would assist counsel in dealing with the client, take notes at the hearing and advise the client after the hearing. The rules have been relaxed over the years to the extent that it is no longer necessary for a solicitor to be present at court with the client. This is a common feature in legal aid cases. If a matter is listed for hearing, a private paying client should be given the option of attending court with counsel but without their solicitor being present. This will save costs for the client. If counsel attends court without a solicitor they are expected to provide a detailed report to their instructing lawyers as to the outcome of the hearing as soon as possible after the hearing.

Direct Access

- The Public Access Rules came into force in July 2004 which permitted members of the public or professional organisations to instruct a barrister directly, without first engaging a Solicitor. In order to represent members of the public on a Direct Access basis, barristers must have undertaken training to the satisfaction of the Bar Standards Board. There will be occasions where it would not be appropriate for a barrister to assist a client directly, in which case he/she will be signposted to a firm of solicitors able to assist.

- The cost of a public access case will depend on the nature of the case. Generally, barristers would work for a fixed fee or alternatively provide an hourly rate if preferred. Services provided by public access barristers include: advisory work, drafting of documents, correspondence, negotiation, court representation.

https://www.barstandardsboard.org.uk/for-the-public/finding-and-using-a-barrister/how-to-instruct-a-barrister/public-access-guidance-for-lay-clients.html

Barristers' Clerk

Barristers' clerks work as administrators within barrister chambers. They keep chamber diaries up-to-date, calculate and negotiate fees for the work carried out and ensure every member is informed of their commitments. Other key responsibilities include allocating cases to barristers, considering their expertise, specialisms and availability, managing financial accounts, marketing the chambers and organising meetings between clients, barristers and instructing Solicitor. Clerks have detailed knowledge about the barristers on their list. In recent years and in line with modernisation of the barristers' profession, some barristers no longer employ clerks but manage their fees and time themselves or use modern management structures.

For more information contact Institute of Barristers' Clerks

https://ibc.org.uk/

When the brief is returned at short notice

A barrister who wishes to return a brief is permitted to do so in enough time to give another barrister a proper opportunity to take over the case. To enable this to happen, a barrister (or more likely his/her clerk) must inform you as soon as they realise there is a possibility that they will be unable to do the work required. This might happen when a barrister has overrun in an earlier case. There are three options in these circumstances: find another barrister, seek an adjournment or take over conduct of the matter. A decision should be made in consultation with your client.

Complaints against barristers

- Circumstances may still arise that require you to consider making a formal complaint against a barrister in relation to his or her professional conduct. As a general rule, you should only invoke those formal complaint procedures after exhausting all informal options to resolve a dispute or difficulty.

- The Bar Standards Board regulates barristers in England and Wales who are responsible for making sure that the high standards of the profession are maintained. There are two ways to make a complaint about a barrister: If the barrister is acting for you and you are not satisfied with their service, you should contact the Legal Ombudsman. http://www.legalombudsman.org.uk/

- If the barrister is not acting for you and you want to complain about their professional conduct, you should contact The Bar Standards Board. http://www.barstandardsboard.org.uk/

CHAPTER 29

FINDING OF FACT HEARINGS

Introduction

- If one party makes allegations during family law proceedings and the other party denies those allegations, the court will consider whether there should be a Fact Finding Hearing. This is a separate hearing arranged to decide whether or not the allegations are true. Fact Finding hearings are most common in children cases, but can also take place during other family law proceedings such as for domestic abuse injunctions or financial remedies.

- At the Fact Finding Hearing the court considers the evidence surrounding allegations made by one party against the other and makes a decision as to whether alleged incidents did or did not happen. The parties give evidence in the witness box and are cross-examined. After having heard the evidence, the Judge or Lay Magistrates will decide whether the alleged incidents happened or not. Most commonly, these allegations concern domestic abuse but can relate to other aspects of behaviour. It is for the party making the allegations to prove that they are true. The Judge or Lay Magistrates will consider on the balance of probabilities whether it is more likely than not that the allegations are true.

Reasons for a Fact Finding Hearing

- The decision about whether to hold a Fact Finding Hearing is for the court not Cafcass or the parties. At the first hearing of the private children application (FHDRA) the court has to consider

Practice Direction 12J Child Arrangements & Contact Orders: Domestic Abuse and Harm (**PD12J**), which informs the court how it should approach cases involving allegations of domestic abuse. The thrust of *PD12J* is that if disputed allegations could be potentially relevant to the decision the court is to make about the child, the court should determine the dispute by deciding whether the allegations are true or not. The decision about whether or not to hold a fact finding hearing should generally be taken early.

- The purpose of this Practice Direction is to assist the Family Court in its decision making when a party alleges she/he has experienced domestic abuse perpetrated by another party.

- The general principles are set out in **Paragraphs 4-8. Practice Direction 12J Practice Direction 12J Child Arrangements & Contact Orders: Domestic Abuse and Harm** is set out in full in the Appendix to this book

Scott Schedule

- In preparation for a Fact Finding Hearing, the party making the allegations will be directed to serve a list of the allegations in the form of a *Scott Schedule*. The list should be signed and dated, each incident should be numbered and set out in date order stating the date of the incident and details of what happened and where, details of any witnesses to the incident and involvement of the police and/or medical services. The list should contain a statement that it is true. The person against whom the allegations are made will be directed to respond to the allegations. The person accused should respond to each allegation in turn, setting out their account of the incident or stating that the allegation is denied. Both parties will also be asked to make written statements setting out their evidence. Witnesses can also make a statement and give evidence with the court's permission.

- If a party has been directed to serve or respond to a Scott Schedule a template form can be used which includes:

- Heading – as with all of court documents

- Number – number the allegations

- Date – date that the incident or behaviour has occurred. If the behaviour happened on more than one occasion dates can be listed. If the behaviour has taken place over a period of time insert when it started and ended. If the abuse is still taking place state 'Ongoing from (date abuse started) until now.'

- Allegations – keep these short and factual. The details of the incidents will be in the party's statement.

- Reference – state where the details of the allegation are in the court bundle

- Refer to any other supporting evidence, for example from the Police, Local Authority or medical records so that the Judge can easily find all the evidence available

- Response – this section is for the other (accused) party to put their response to each allegation. The party preparing the schedule leaves this part blank for the other party to fill in. They will need to say whether they admit or deny the allegations. If they deny an allegation it means they do not agree that it happened. The person responding to the allegation will also need to refer to any evidence they have provided on the allegation

- Judge's finding – leave a column in the table for the Judge to complete at court. The Judge will hear evidence and decide whether they find each allegation to be true. If the Judge finds that an allegation is true he/she will state that the allegation is found. If the Judge decides that the allegation is not true he/she will state that the allegation is not found. If the Judge cannot decide whether the allegation is true or not he/she may state that the allegation cannot be determined either way

- Sign, print name and date the schedule

Witness Statements

- Each party must prepare a witness statement. Usually the person making the allegations goes first. Each allegation or incident will be dealt with by the parties. Sometimes the court will place a limit on the number of allegations that should be included in the schedule of allegations to ensure that the case is manageable and the Fact Finding Hearing is focused on the most relevant issues.

The Fact Finding Hearing Itself

The general format of a Fact Finding Hearing will be as follows:

- The person making allegations of abuse (and his/her witnesses) will give evidence first. The party will confirm (or correct) their witness statement and may then be asked questions by or on behalf of the other party. Sometimes the Judge will ask some questions.

- The same process then happens for the person who is accused of abuse and any witnesses he/she has brought to court.

- The parties (or their Solicitor if they have one) will then be able to make submissions, to the Judge.

- The Judge will announce the decision and give reasons.

This process might vary if one or both parties has no Solicitor and the court makes special arrangements because of that.

Statutory changes

- The **Domestic Abuse Act 2021** came into force on 29 April 2021. For the family courts, there are several implications, in particular, provision for protection for victims and witnesses in legal proceedings: The prohibition on cross-examination in person by those alleged to be victims or perpetrators of domestic abuse (**section 65 Domestic Abuse Act 2021**).

- This subject is highly relevant in finding of fact hearings. The removal of legal aid for many private family law cases means that one or both parties are unrepresented in a large number of cases. The prohibition of cross-examination is introduced through an amendment to the Matrimonial and Family Proceedings Act 1984 by insertion of 31Q-31Z which came into force on the 21st July 2022.

- Under the **Domestic Abuse Act 2021** there can be prohibition on cross-examination in four circumstances:

    First, there is a prohibition for cross-examination by a party who has been convicted, cautioned, or is charged with a specified offence. It will also prevent victims of domestic abuse (or a specified offence) from having to cross-examine a witness who has been convicted, cautioned or charged with that offence. The specified offences will be defined in the regulation, which is not yet in place.

    Second, there is a prohibition on cross-examination by a party subject to an on-notice protective injunction. This also extends to parties who are protected by an on-notice injunction.

    The third category includes a similar prohibition on cross-examination, but where there is 'specified evidence' of domestic abuse.

The fourth category is a safety valve where none of the above applies. In the absence of applicability of any of the above, the Court will have the power to prohibit a party from cross-examining a witness in person if:

- The quality condition or the significant distress condition is met; and

- It is not contrary to the interest of justice to give the direction.

The quality condition is met if the quality of the evidence is likely to be diminished if cross-examined by the party in person, and the quality of the evidence would be improved if the direction were given under the section.

Where any of the above conditions are met, the Court will consider if there are any alternative means for the witness to be cross-examined. In cases when the Court considers there is no alternative, the Court must invite the party to the proceedings to arrange for a legal representative and require the party to notify the Court, by the end of a period specified by the Court, whether a legal representative is to act for the party. If the party has notified that they will not have a legal representative or has not notified at all, then the Court will consider if it is necessary in the interests of justice for the witness to be cross-examined by a qualified legal representative appointed by the Court to represent the interest of the party. If the Court decides that it is in the interest of justice, the Court must appoint a legal representative chosen by the Court to cross-examine the witness. The Lord Chancellor has made provision for payment to legal representatives to be made out of central funds.

Future changes to procedure

Following the cases in the Court of Appeal of **Re H-N and Others (children) (domestic abuse: finding of fact hearings) [2021] EWCA Civ 448** the court stated:

1. *It is accepted by the court, the parties and within the two reports, that PD12J remains fit for the purpose for which it was designed, namely to provide the courts with a structure enabling the court first to recognise all forms of domestic abuse and thereafter on how to approach such allegations when made in private law proceedings*

2. Specific guidance was given by the court in relation to:

- *Whether there should be a finding of fact hearing*

The proper approach ... emphasises the need to consider the nature of the allegations, the relevance to the decision to be made in relation to the child, and the need for the court to decide if a fact-finding hearing is 'necessary and proportionate';

- *The use of Scott Schedules.*

The court endorsed the view ... that the time has come for there to be a move away from Scott Schedules as a means of identifying issues to be tried by the Family Court. Scott Schedules, which identify specific factual incidents tied to a particular date and time, are at risk of failing to focus on the wider context and whether there has been a pattern of coercive and controlling behaviour;

- *The approach to controlling and coercive behaviour.*

The court emphasised the need to evaluate the existence or otherwise of a pattern of coercive and controlling behaviour without significantly increasing the scale and length of private law proceedings, in circumstances where delay is inimical to the welfare of a child and the courts;

- *The relevance of criminal law concepts*

Whilst the Family Courts and the parties who appear in them should not shy away from using words such as 'rape' in the manner in which they are used in ordinary speech, the law is clear that criminal law concepts should not be imported to the Family court. There is a distinction between judges needing to understand the potential psychological impact of sexual assault on a victim on the one hand and the importance of Family judges avoiding being drawn into an analysis of factual evidence based on criminal law proceedings on the other.

It should be stressed that the guidance given by the Court of Appeal in these cases has no formal legal authority at present but it is likely that changes are likely to be made on these issues in due course.

The case of **AA v BB [2021] EWHC 1822 (Fam)** considered the implications of **Re H-N**. In that case the appeal was against a case management decision to exclude evidence from a fact finding hearing. The mother relied on the dicta of the Court of Appeal in **Re H-N** regarding **the limitations** of Scott Schedules and the fact that the court focused on particular allegations **rather than** looking at patterns of overall behaviour.

The Court of Appeal then heard the case of **K v K [2022] EWCA 468** which states ' This judgement is intended to provide general guidance on the proper approach to fact-finding hearings in private family proceedings following this courts decision in **Re H-N**.

A summary of the principles of **K v K** are these:

a. the nature of the allegations **and the extent** to which those allegations are likely to to relevant **to the making of the child arrangements order;**

b. that the purpose of fact finding is to allow **assessment of the risk to the child** and the **impact** of any abuse on the child;

c. whether fact finding **is necessary** or whether other evidence suffices and;

d. whether fact finding is **proportionate**.

The court expressed concern that a perception had formed that **Re H-N** created a requirement that in every case in which allegations of domestic abuse are made, the court should conduct a fact finding exercise with a detailed analysis of each specific allegation. The Court of Appeal reiterated that the courts duty is limited to determining determining factual disputes that are likely to be relevant to deciding how to make a child arrangements order.

The emphasis now placed by the Court of Appeal on the relevance and effect of disputed facts was expressed simply at para 45: 'without in anyway resiling from what was said at [139] of *Re H-N* about the pernicious nature of domestic abuse, fact-finding is only needed if the alleged abuse is likely to be relevant to what the court is being asked to decide relating to the children's welfare.

This case sends a signal to family courts to be discerning when deciding on *the need* to have a fact finding hearing.

CHAPTER 30

CAFCASS AND LOCAL AUTHORITY REPORTS

Private law proceedings are initiated by a party with parental responsibility applying to the court for a Child Arrangements Order or other Section 8 order using a C100 application form. Within the C100 application form is a box which can be ticked in order to alert the court that there has been previous local authority involvement. The form is placed on the court file and a copy is sent to the parties and to the Children and Family Court Advisory and Support Service (Cafcass) an independent organisation tasked with looking after the interests of children involved in family proceedings.

Safeguarding Letter.

About two to three weeks before the first hearing, known as a First Hearing and Dispute Resolution Appointment [FHDRA], Cafcass will complete their safeguarding checks. An important feature of the safeguarding letter is to outline what recommendations Cafcass make to the court and whether and to what extent there has been local authority involvement with the family. Safeguarding checks are also undertaken with the police to find out whether there are any known relevant criminal convictions, and to the Local Authority to ascertain whether there are any safety or welfare risks to the child. Cafcass will also speak to the parties over the telephone. The results of these enquiries are included in the Safeguarding Letter as well as guidance to the court as to how to progress the case. A Cafcass Officer attends the FHDRA and can speak to parties to clarify any issues and wherever possible, conduct an early dispute resolution to see whether agreement can be reached or the issues narrowed.

Section 7 Reports

- Under s7(1) of the Children Act 1989, a court considering any question with respect to a child under this Act may –

    (a) ask an officer of the Service or a Welsh family proceedings officer; or

    (b) ask a local authority to arrange for –

    (i) an officer of the authority; or

    (ii) such other person (other than an officer of the Service or a Welsh family proceedings officer) as the authority considers appropriate, to report to the court on such matters relating to the welfare of that child as are required to be dealt with in the report.

- In accordance with Practice Direction 12B, paragraph 14(b), section 7 reports should only be ordered in cases where there is a dispute as to with whom the child should live, spend time, or otherwise have contact with. A report can also be ordered:

    (i) If there is an issue concerning the child's wishes, and/or

    (ii) If there is an alleged risk to the child, and/or

    (iii) Where information and advice is needed which the court considers to be necessary before a decision can be reached in the case.

- As a matter of course, these reports are completed by Cafcass. However, as section 7 makes clear, the court can direct the Local Authority to prepare this report where the local authority has been involved previously or where the court is considering an alleged risk to the child.

- A Section 7 Children Act 1989 report is a report written by a Cafcass worker or a social worker from the Local Authority in cases where it has had a recent involvement with the family in question.

- A Section 7 report may be required in private proceedings where an application has been made to the court for an order under Section 8 Children Act 1989, which may be:

  - Child Arrangements Order – specifies whom the child is to live with and/or with whom the child is to have contact;

  - Prohibited Steps Order – prevents either parent from doing certain things or making specific trips with their children without the express permission of the other parent;

  - Specific Issue Order – an order to determine a specific question which has or may arise in connection with any aspect in relation to a child;

  - Family Assistance Order – a short-term order requiring a Cafcass officer or a social worker to advise, assist, and befriend any person in the named order.

- A Section 7 report is only ordered by the court when it needs information about a child's welfare, what is best for the child and sometimes where there are certain risk factors or concerns raised in relation to a child, parent or other relative.

- A Cafcass worker or social worker will provide an independent assessment of a situation and will report these findings to the court. The author of the report may be required to attend court in support of the report but only if the court directs such attendance.

- The court usually stipulates what it requires Cafcass or the social worker to focus on in their report.

Contents of Section 7 Report

- A Section 7 report should contain all background information, key facts and evidence stipulated in accordance with the Welfare Checklist. The report will set out the child's wishes and feelings and what the Cafcass officer or Local Authority social worker considers to be in the best interest of the child.

- The worker who prepares the report may speak to the child (depending on their age and understanding) about his/her wishes and feelings and what he/she would like to happen.

- They will also spend time with both parties and listen to any concerns they may have. They may also speak to others such as family members, teachers and health workers. They will not ask the child to make a decision or to choose between either parent regarding with whom they will live or the contact they will have with the non-resident parent.

Decision and Court Order

After reading the report and listening to what the parties and other people in the case have said, the court will make the final decision on the court application. This decision will be based on what is best for the child. It will take into account the wishes and feelings of the child only if this is considered to be in their best interests. The decision will be set out in a court order with which the parties must comply.

Rule 16.4 Appointments

Rule 16.4 of the FPR provides that, without prejudice to rule 8.42 (Application for consent to marriage or civil partnership of a child) or rule 16.6 (circumstances in which a child does not need a guardian), the court must appoint a children's guardian for a child who is the subject of proceedings, which are not specified proceedings or adoption proceedings, if –

(a) the child is an applicant in the proceedings;

(b) a provision in these rules provides for the child to be a party to the proceedings; or

(c) the court has made the child a party in accordance with rule 16.2.

Child as a party to proceedings

- Under rule 16.2(1), the court may make a child a party to proceedings if it considers it is in the best interests of the child to do so.

- Practice direction 16A provides guidance on when a child should be made a party to proceedings. Paragraph 7.1 emphasises that this step should only be taken in cases of significant difficulty and consideration should be given to whether an alternative route may be preferable e.g. making a referral to social services.

- Paragraph 7.2 offers guidance on the situations where it may be appropriate to make a child a party to proceedings. This paragraph stresses that this list is provided as guidance only and that the decision to make the child a party will always be exclusively that of the court, made in the light of the facts and circumstances of the particular case.

- The situations outlined in paragraph 7.2 are as follows;

    (a) where an officer of the Service or Welsh family proceedings officer has notified the court that in the opinion of that officer the child should be made a party;

(b) where the child has a standpoint or interest which is inconsistent with or incapable of being represented by any of the adult parties;

(c) where there is an intractable dispute over residence or contact, including where all contact has ceased, or where there is irrational but implacable hostility to contact or where the child may be suffering harm associated with the contact dispute;

(d) where the views and wishes of the child cannot be adequately met by a report to the court;

(e) where an older child is opposing a proposed course of action;

(f) where there are complex medical or mental health issues to be determined or there are other unusually complex issues that necessitate separate representation of the child;

(g) where there are international complications outside child abduction, in particular where it may be necessary for there to be discussions with overseas authorities or a foreign court;

(h) where there are serious allegations of physical, sexual or other abuse in relation to the child or there are allegations of domestic violence not capable of being resolved with the help of an officer of the Service or Welsh family proceedings officer;

(i) where the proceedings concern more than one child and the welfare of the children is in conflict or one child is in a particularly disadvantaged position;

(j) where there is a contested issue about scientific testing.

- Pursuant to paragraph 7.3, the court must take into account the risk of delay or other factors adverse to the child in deciding whether to make the child a party to proceedings. The court's primary consideration will be the best interests of the child.

- In relation to articulate teenagers, the court must take into account their right to freedom of expression and participation. Sir James Munby in the case of **Cambra v Jones and another [2014] All ER (D) 30 (Apr)** cited with approval the view expressed by Thorpe LJ at paragraph 28 of his judgment in **Mabon v Mabon [2005] EWCA Civ 634**:

   "We must, in the case of articulate teenagers, accept that the right to freedom of expression and participation outweighs the paternalistic judgment of welfare."

- In relation to Hague Convention proceedings, Baroness Hale commented at paragraph 60 of her judgment in the case of **Re D (a child) [2006] UKHL 51** that full scale legal representation of a child will only be necessary in a few cases but that the child should be represented "whenever it seems likely that the child's views and interests may not be properly presented to the court, and in particular where there are legal arguments which the adult parties are not putting forward".

Rule 16.4 of the Family Procedure Rules 2010 and Practice Direction 16A allows a child to be made a party in family proceedings and obtain legal representation in their own right. The decision to make the child a party will always be **exclusively that of the court**, made in the light of the facts and circumstances of the particular case. That decision will not normally be taken by the court without first taking account of the views of Cafcass.

Before making the child a party, consideration should be given to whether an alternative route might be preferable, such as asking Cafcass to carry out further work or by making a referral to Social Services or by obtaining expert evidence.

The court may consider making a child party to proceedings if it is satisfied that the case meets one or more of the following criteria:

- where a Family Court Advisor has recommended the child should be made a party

- the dispute between the adult parties is such that the interests of the child are not being met

- where there is an intractable dispute or where there is implacable hostility to contact or where the child may be suffering harm associated with the contact dispute

- where the views and wishes of the child cannot be adequately met by a Section 7 Report to the court

- where an older child is opposing a proposed course of action

- where there are complex issues that necessitate separate representation of the child

- where there are international elements to the case which may necessitate discussions with overseas authorities or a foreign court

- where there are serious allegations of abuse to the child and/or allegations of domestic violence

- where the proceedings concern more than one child and the welfare of the children is in conflict or one child is in a particularly disadvantaged position

- where there is a contested issue about scientific testing.

The Children's Guardian appointed to represent the child will

- Instruct a solicitor who specialises in Family Law and is on the Law Society Children's Panel to act for the child

- Meet with the child and the parties in the proceedings

- If age appropriate, obtain the child's wishes and feelings

- Advise the court about any work, including extra services such as expert opinions, that they believe are necessary to assist the court

- If directed by the court, write a report for the court and attend appropriate court hearings

- Provide expert advice to the court and make recommendations as to what is considered to be in the child's best interests.

Section 37 Reports

Section 37 of the Children Act 1989 provides that:

(1) Where, in any family proceedings in which a question arises with respect to the welfare of any child, it appears to the court that it may be appropriate for a care or supervision order to be made with respect to him, the court may direct the appropriate authority to undertake an investigation of the child's circumstances.

(2) Where the court gives a direction under this section the local authority concerned shall, when undertaking the investigation, consider whether they should –

    (a) apply for a care order or for a supervision order with respect to the child;

    (b) provide services or assistance for the child or his family; or

(c) take any other action with respect to the child.

An order under s37 compels the local authority to seriously consider whether care proceedings should be issued and forces them to justify any decision not to do so (s37(3)(a)). This direction involves a very high level of local authority involvement as, even if they do not issue care proceedings, their report must set out any service or assistance which they have provided, or to intend to provide, for the child and his family (s37(3)(b)) and any other action which they have taken, or propose to take, with respect to the child (s37(3)©). The local authority's conclusions under s37 will influence the future course of proceedings and what orders the court ultimately makes.

If the local authority ultimately decided not to issue proceedings, the court has no power to make a care order or supervision order of its own motion (as per Sir Stephen Brown P in **Nottinghamshire County Council v P [1993] EWCA Civ 35**)

The court has the power under **s38(1)(b)** of the Children Act 1989 to make an interim care order or supervision order while a s37 investigation is ongoing.

Pursuant to **s38(2)**, the court shall not make an interim care order or interim supervision order under this section unless it is satisfied that there are reasonable grounds for believing that circumstances with respect to the child are as mentioned in **section 31(2)**, namely;

(a) that the child concerned is suffering, or is likely to suffer, significant harm; and

(b) that the harm, or likelihood of harm, is attributable to –

    (i) the care given to the child, or likely to be given to him if the order were not made, not being what it would be reasonable to expect a parent to give to him; or

(ii) the child's being beyond parental control.

If the local authority decides to issue proceedings for a care or supervision order, these proceedings will take priority over existing private law proceedings. Under **s9(1) of the Children Act 1989** no court shall make a child arrangements order with respect to a child who is in the care of the local authority, other than an order relating to who the child is to live with and when the child is to live with any person.

Family Assistance Orders

Within the private law proceedings, there can also be Family Assistance Orders ('FAO') pursuant to **s 16 Children Act 1989** which can be a recommendation that the local authority make within the s 7 report in conjunction with a private law order.

A direction for a FAO can be made requiring a Cafcass officer or a social worker within a local authority to be made available to advise, assist, befriend any person named in the order. That person could be a person with whom the child lives such as a parent, a guardian or the children themselves and the order can be made to last for up to 12 months.

Before a FAO can be made, every person named in the order (apart from the child) must consent and a FAO therefore cannot be made against a local authority unless they agree and the child concerned lives or will live within their area (s 16(7)).

The assistance contained within a FAO is similar to that of a supervision order, however there is no need for any threshold to be established as there would be within the context of a public law order.

CHAPTER 31

LITIGANTS IN PERSON & MCKENZIE FRIENDS IN FAMILY PROCEEDINGS

- Litigant in Person is the term which should be used in all criminal, civil and family courts to describe individuals who exercise their right to conduct legal proceedings on their own behalf.

- The number of Litigants in Person has risen significantly in recent years and is likely to continue to do so as a result of financial constraints and the consequences of the Legal Aid reforms. Public funding in private law family proceedings is now available in only exceptional circumstances.

- 'Those who exercise a personal right to conduct proceedings themselves, operate in what feels like an alien environment. All too often, the Litigant in Person is regarded as a problem for Judges and for the Court system rather than a person for whom the system of Civil Justice exists' (**Lord Woolf Access to Justice, Interim Report June 1995**).

Rules and Practice in Litigant in Person cases

A Solicitor has a duty to his/her client, a duty to the court and the administration of justice, and a duty to assist (within limits) a Litigant in Person.

The professional and regulatory framework

A lawyer's paramount duty is to the court and to the administration of justice.

The Legal Services Act 2007 s1(3)

> *referring to lawyers as 'authorised persons', provides that...authorised persons should act in the best interests of their client,*
>
> *(d) ...persons who exercise before any court a right of audience, or conduct litigation in relation to proceedings in any court, by virtue of being authorised persons should comply with their duty to the court to act with independence in the interests of justice...'*
>
> *That duty may operate to the potential disadvantage of a lawyer's client by, for example, requiring that the Solicitor should not mislead the court or withhold from it, documents and authorities even when they detract from the client's case. Subject to that, a lawyer's duty is to their client.*

Chartered Institute of Legal Executives Regulation

The Chartered Institute of Legal Executives Regulation Code of Conduct is available at https://www.cilex.org.uk/about_cilex/the_code_of_conduct/. It applies to their members, practitioners and Authorised Entities.

It provides that they must:

> '1. Uphold the rule of law and the impartial administration of justice:
>
> *1.1 Understand and comply with your primary and overriding duty to the court, obey court orders and do nothing which would place you in contempt.*
>
> *1.2 Not knowingly or recklessly allow the court to be misled.*

2.2 Not engage in any conduct that could undermine or affect adversely the confidence and trust placed in you and your profession by your client, your employer, professional colleagues, the public and others'.

Rule 4 of the CILEx Rights of Audience Conduct Rules provides: *'CILEx advocates have a primary and an overriding duty to the court to ensure in the public interest, that the proper and efficient administration of justice is achieved. They must assist the court in the administration of justice and must not deceive the court or knowingly or recklessly mislead it'.*

Rule 5 provides that: 'CILEx advocates must not engage in conduct, whether in the exercise of their rights of audience or otherwise, which is:

(a) dishonest or otherwise discreditable to an advocate;

(b) prejudicial to the administration of justice; or

(c) likely to diminish public confidence in the legal profession or the administration of justice, or otherwise bring the legal profession into disrepute'.

Bar Standards Board

Every barrister is bound by the core duties in the Bar Standards Board Handbook (the 'BSB Handbook') which can be found online at https://www.barstandardsboard.org.uk/for-barristers/bsb-handbook-and-code-guidance/the-bsb-handbook.html. The guidance at **gC1** identifies when particular duties may take precedence over others. This includes the statement at **gC1.1** that the duty to the court in the administration of justice overrides any other core duty, if and to the extent that the two are inconsistent.

Rule C3 states: *'You owe a duty to the court to act with independence in the interests of justice. This duty overrides any inconsistent obligations which you may have (other than obligations under the criminal law).*

It includes the following specific obligations which apply whether the barrister is acting as an advocate or is otherwise involved in the conduct of litigation in whatever role (with the exception of rule C3.1 below, which applies when acting as an advocate):

- *you must not knowingly or recklessly mislead or attempt to mislead the court;*

- *you must not abuse your role as an advocate;*

- *you must take reasonable steps to avoid wasting the court's time;*

- *you must take reasonable steps to ensure that the court has before it, all relevant decisions and legislative provisions; and*

- *you must ensure that your ability to act independently is not compromised.*

Rule C4 states: *'Your duty to act in the best interests of each client is subject to your duty to the court'.*

The BSB Handbook also makes this specific reference to Litigant in Person: *'gC5 Your duty under rule C3.3 includes drawing to the attention of the court any decision or provision which may be adverse to the interests of your client. It is particularly important where you are appearing against a litigant who is not legally represented'.*

If a barrister is contacted directly by a Litigant in Person, the barrister's clerk or the barrister himself should let the Litigant in Person know whether it is appropriate for the Litigant in Person to speak with the barrister or the solicitor.

Barristers must still exercise their professional independence about this issue and have regard to the best interests of their client. For example, if the purpose of the discussion is related to the conduct of the litigation, referral to the instructing solicitor (or the client in a public access case) would be appropriate. If the communication is related to the barrister's role as advocate, the barrister would be entitled to refer the communication to the solicitor (or client), but it may be appropriate for the barrister to communicate with the Litigant in Person directly, particularly if the issues are matters that ordinarily would be discussed between barristers.

Solicitors Regulation Authority (SRA)

Chapter 5 of the Solicitors Regulation Authority Handbook says:

The SRA Standards and Regulations can be found online at https://www.sra.org.uk/sra/how-we-work/privacy-data-information/disclosure-policy/publication/ and note that solicitors' client care obligations under the SRA regulations apply as much to 'unbundled' services as they do to a full retainer.

Knowing and using law and procedure effectively against your opponent because you have the skills to do so, whether that be against a qualified representative or a Litigant in Person, is not taking 'unfair advantage' or a breach of any regulatory code.

Summary

- There is a paramount duty to the court and the administration of justice.

- That duty to the court will take precedence if it conflicts with a duty to a client.

- A Solicitor must not take unfair advantage of a Litigant in Person.

- There is no obligation to help a Litigant in Person to run their case or to take any action on a Litigant in Person's behalf. By doing so the Solicitor might be failing in his duties to his own client. *Khudados v Hayden [2007] EWCA Civ 1316@ paragraph 38*

Costs and Litigants in Person

Litigants in Person (Costs and Expenses) Act 1975 (as amended) gives a Litigant in Person the right to recover sums in respect of any work done, and any expenses and losses incurred, by a litigant in or in connection with the proceedings to which the order relates.

This Act applies all civil and family courts and establishes the principle that a costs order can be made against a represented party. The mechanics of how this works in practice are found in the Civil Procedure Rules

Under **rule 46.5 of the Civil Procedure Rules** which apply to family proceedings (**Family Procedure Rules 28.2**) the court may award a litigant in person their costs.

Whilst neither the 1975 Act nor the Civil Procedure Rules (CPR) defines a Litigant in Person, **CPR 46.5(6)** states that a Litigant in Person can include a company or other corporation, a barrister, a solicitor, a solicitor's employee, a manager of a body recognised under **section 9 of the Administration of Justice Act** 1985 (incorporated practices) and a person who, for the purposes of the **Legal Services Act 2007**, is authorised to conduct litigation.

This means that a person who acts on his own behalf for either all or part of the claim is likely to be a Litigant in Person, unless represented. However, the fact that legal representation may be for only part of the proceedings does not preclude a successful Litigant in Person from recovering costs for the aspect of work he conducted while not represented **Agassi v Robinson (HM Inspector of Taxes) [2005] EWCA Civ 1507**. In **Agassi** the costs of employing a tax expert to undertake litigation work were not recoverable as a disbursement since a legal representative would not have employed a third party to undertake such work.

Family Courts have not generally made orders for costs, except in extreme cases, and they are often unwilling to make orders for costs against unrepresented parties.

Courts have sympathised with unrepresented parties as they are not being represented by a trained Solicitor. However, in *Veluppillai v Veluppillai* [2015] EWHC 3095 (Fam) a costs order was made against an unrepresented party.

Cost orders can be awarded against a party if they fail to adhere to Court directions, make unwarranted applications, or generally conduct themselves in an unreasonable manner.

Further information

Resolution: Good Practice Guide to Working with Litigants in Person

https://resolution.org.uk/resolutions-good-practice-guides/good-practice-guide-to-working-with-litigants-in-person/

Resolution top tips for members working with Litigant in Person

https://resolution.org.uk/top-tips-for-members-working-with-lips/

A Handbook for Litigants in Person Courts and Tribunals Judiciary

https://www.judiciary.uk/wp-content/uploads/JCO/Documents/Guidance/A_Handbook_for_Litigants_in_Person.pdf

Guidelines for Lawyers dealing with Litigant in Person

https://prdsitecore93.azureedge.net/-/media/files/topics/family-and-children/litigants-in-person-guidelines-lawyers-june-2015.pdf

A Practical Guide to Working with Litigants in Person and McKenzie Friends in Family Cases https://www.amazon.co.uk/Practical-Working-Litigants-McKenzie-Friends/dp/1912687674/

Particular help for a Litigant in Person

- **Support Through Court (previously the Personal Support Unit)** is available in certain courts round the country. These courts offer help to unrepresented parties (a Litigant in Person) involved in civil and family proceedings Often, the bigger the court, the more likely there is such help for the unrepresented party. The Personal Support Unit is a charity staffed largely by volunteers. They cannot give legal advice as they are not legally trained but they can offer practical and emotional support to people facing a court without a Solicitor, including help with completing the court forms. Information can be provided as to where legal advice can be found. The volunteer can accompany the Litigant in Person whilst in court but cannot speak on their behalf. The service is free of charge.

- **Barrister Direct Access**

Anyone can now go directly to a barrister, for advice and/or representation, without having to involve anyone else. Barristers can advise a Litigant in Person on their legal status and rights. Barristers can draft and send documents for the Litigant in Person and represent him/her in court. The main advantage of the Direct Access Scheme for consumers of legal services is the opportunity to save on legal costs, specifically solicitor's fees. However, removing solicitors from the process of running a legal case often requires that clients themselves must perform the majority of document management, filing, and other related activities in the context of conducting litigation. Barristers are not allowed to take on direct access clients unless doing so is in both the client's best interests and in the interests of justice. In complicated cases, barristers must recommend to clients that they obtain external support from a solicitor. However, since the expense of using a solicitor can potentially defeat the cost-saving purpose of the Direct Access Scheme, consumers have the option of using a provider of Public Access Legal Support Service

(PALS), which is a specialised paralegal resource catering to barristers and clients who work together within the framework of the Direct Access Scheme. This service is, of course, available to a Litigant in Person in family proceedings.

- **Qualified legal representatives**

Under the Domestic Abuse Act 2021 there can be prohibition on personal cross-examination by a Litigant in Person in four circumstances:

First, there is a prohibition for cross-examination by a party who has been convicted, cautioned, or is charged with a specified offence. It will also prevent victims of domestic abuse (or a specified offence) from having to cross-examine a witness who has been convicted, cautioned or charged with that offence. The specified offences will be defined in the regulation, which is not yet in place.

Second, there will be a prohibition on cross-examination by a party subject to an on-notice protective injunction. This also extends to parties who are protected by an on-notice injunction. What constitutes "protective injunctions" will be defined in a regulation yet to be issued by the Lord Chancellor.

The third category includes a similar prohibition on cross-examination, but where there is 'specified evidence' of domestic abuse.

The fourth category is a safety valve where none of the above applies. In the absence of applicability of any of the above, the Court will have the power to prohibit a party from cross-examining a witness in person if:

- The quality condition or the significant distress condition is met; and

- It is not contrary to the interest of justice to give the direction.

The quality condition is met if the quality of the evidence is likely to be diminished if cross-examined by the party in person, and the quality of the evidence would be improved if the direction were given under the section.

The significant distress condition is met if it would cause significant distress to the witness or the party, and that distress is likely to be more significant than would be the case if the witness were cross-examined other than by the party in person.

Where any of the above conditions are met, the Court will consider if there are any alternative means for the witness to be cross-examined or of obtaining evidence that the witness might have given under cross-examination.

In cases when the Court considers there is no alternative, the Court must invite the party to the proceedings to arrange for a legal representative and require the party to notify the Court, by the end of a period specified by the Court, whether a legal representative is to act for the party.

If the party has notified that they will not have a legal representative or has not notified at all, then the Court will consider if it is necessary in the interests of justice for the witness to be cross-examined by a Qualified Legal Representative appointed by the Court to represent the interest of the party. If the court decides that it is in the interest of justice, the court must appoint a legal representative chosen by the court to cross-examine the witness. This provision applies to applications filed on or after 21st July 2022

CASE LAW

Recent civil and family decisions show that a Litigant in Person is not able to blame non-compliance with important legal provisions merely on their unrepresented status.

An important decision underlining this point is **Barton v Wright Hassall LLP [2018] UKSC 12**. In this case, a Litigant in Person issued a claim form and elected to serve this on the defendant himself. On the last day prior to the deadline for service of the claim form, the claimant emailed the defendant's solicitors, attaching the claim form by way of service. However, he had not obtained permission from them to serve the claim form electronically, and he was subsequently informed that as they had not indicated that they would accept service by email, the claim form had expired and the action was now statute-barred. The claimant made an application for an order validating service retrospectively, and this proceeded to the highest appellate court.

The Supreme Court found that, although in the current climate of cuts to legal aid, acting as a Litigant in Person was not always by choice, "it will not usually justify applying to litigants in person a lower standard of compliance with rules or orders of the court".

The Civil Procedure Rules provide a framework within which to balance the interests of both sides, and if a Litigant in Person was entitled to greater indulgence in complying with these rules then this would affect that balance. Unless the rules in question were "particularly inaccessible or obscure", a Litigant in Person should familiarise himself with any relevant rules which apply. The rules in this instance were not inaccessible or obscure, and so the claimant's appeal was dismissed.

The Supreme Court also stated that although the defendant's solicitors could have warned the claimant that they did not accept service by email, they were under no duty to do so.

No special treatment by the court

Tinkler v Elliott (2012) EWCA Civ 1289

The self-representing Mr Elliott failed to attend a hearing but instead submitted a medical certificate of unfitness to attend court. The High Court set aside the judgement holding that Mr Elliott had a good reason for not attending the original hearing. The Court of Appeal restored the original court's decision holding that the court rules need to be rigorously applied and that there were no special rules for a Litigant in Person

Jones v Longley & Others (2015) EWHC 3362 (Ch)

The court said that a Litigant in Person is not subject to any special rules and is as liable as represented litigants to have costs orders made against them.

Barton v Wright Hassall LLP (2018) UKSC Civ 12

The Supreme Court decided that the civil procedure rules would not be applied differently to unrepresented litigants. While the court could offer leeway in how litigants were handled during case management hearings or during the trial, this would not usually justify applying a lower standard of compliance with rules or orders of the court The court also indicated that solicitors should not be expected to flag up procedural mistakes made by a Litigant in Person on the other side.

A Litigant in Person is expected to comply with all the court rules and procedures as confirmed in **Barton v Wright Hassell** but there will often be a need to take a more flexible approach in family cases as stated by Munby LJ in **Re C [2012] EWCA Civ 1489.**

In *Ameyaw v McGoldrick & Ors* [2020] EWHC 1741 (QB) the Judge refused a McKenzie Friend permission to speak on behalf of a litigant, stressing the Claimant was well-educated and clearly able to speak on her own behalf.

Judges, Lawyers and the Litigant in Person

According to the most recent version of **The Equal Treatment Bench Book**, at any court hearing a Judge should aim to ensure that Litigants in Person understand what is going on and what is expected of them at all stages of the proceedings. More often than not, the Judge treads a fine line between making sure a hearing is productive and worthwhile, whilst at the same time, ensuring that the unrepresented party has a fair and proper hearing.

Practice Guidance: McKenzie Friends (Civil and Family Courts) dated the 12 July 2010 still stands as current authority:

1) This Guidance applies to civil and family proceedings in the Court of Appeal (Civil Division), the High Court of Justice, the County Courts and the Family Proceedings Court in the Magistrates' Courts. It is issued as guidance (**not** as a Practice Direction) by the Master of the Rolls, as Head of Civil Justice, and the President of the Family Division, as Head of Family Justice. It is intended to remind courts and litigants of the principles set out in the authorities and supersedes the guidance contained in *Practice Note (Family Courts: McKenzie Friends) (No 2)* [2008] 1 WLR 2757, which is now withdrawn. It is issued in light of the increase in litigants-in-person (litigants) in all levels of the civil and family courts.

The Right to Reasonable Assistance

2) Litigants have the right to have reasonable assistance from a layperson, sometimes called a McKenzie Friend (MF). Litigants assisted by MFs remain litigants-in-person. MFs have no independent right to provide assistance. They have no right to act as advocates or to carry out the conduct of litigation.

What McKenzie Friends may do

3) MFs may: i) provide moral support for litigants; ii) take notes; iii) help with case papers; iii) quietly give advice on any aspect of the conduct of the case.

What McKenzie Friends may not do

4) MFs may not: i) act as the litigants' agent in relation to the proceedings; ii) manage litigants' cases outside court, for example by signing court documents; or iii) address the court, make oral submissions or examine witnesses.

Exercising the Right to Reasonable Assistance

5) While litigants ordinarily have a right to receive reasonable assistance from MFs the court retains the power to refuse to permit such assistance. The court may do so where it is satisfied that, in that case, the interests of justice and fairness do not require the litigant to receive such assistance.

6) A litigant who wishes to exercise this right should inform the Judge as soon as possible indicating who the MF will be. The proposed MF should produce a short curriculum vitae or other statement setting out relevant experience, confirming that he or she has no interest in the case and understands the MF's role and the duty of confidentiality.

7) If the court considers that there might be grounds for circumscribing the right to receive such assistance, or a party objects to the presence of, or assistance given by a MF, it is not for the litigant to justify the exercise of the right. It is for the court or the objecting party to provide sufficient reasons why the litigant should not receive such assistance.

8) When considering whether to circumscribe the right to assistance or refuse a MF permission to attend the right to a fair trial is engaged. The matter should be considered carefully. The litigant should be given a reasonable opportunity to argue the point. The proposed MF should not be excluded from that hearing and should normally be allowed to help the litigant.

9) Where proceedings are in *closed court,* i.e.the hearing is in chambers, is in private, or the proceedings relate to a child, the litigant is required to justify the MF's presence in court. The presumption in favour of permitting a MF to attend such hearings, and thereby enable litigants to exercise the right to assistance, is a strong one.

10) The court may refuse to allow a litigant to exercise the right to receive assistance at the start of a hearing. The court can also circumscribe the right during the course of a hearing. It may be refused at the start of a hearing or later circumscribed where the court forms the view that a MF may give, has given, or is giving, assistance which impedes the efficient administration of justice. However, the court should also consider whether a firm and unequivocal warning to the litigant and/or MF might suffice in the first instance.

11) A decision by the court not to curtail assistance from a MF should be regarded as final, save on the ground of subsequent misconduct by the MF or on the ground that the MF's continuing presence will impede the efficient administration of justice. In such event the court should give a short judgment setting out the reasons why it has curtailed the right to assistance. Litigants may appeal such decisions. MFs have no standing to do so.

12) The following factors should not be taken to justify the court refusing to permit a litigant receiving such assistance:

   (i) The case or application is simple or straightforward, or is, for instance, a directions or case management hearing;

   (ii) The litigant appears capable of conducting the case without assistance; (iii) The litigant is unrepresented through choice;

   (iv) The other party is not represented;

(v) The proposed MF belongs to an organisation that promotes a particular cause;

(vi) The proceedings are confidential and the court papers contain sensitive information relating to a family's affairs

13) A litigant may be denied the assistance of a MF because its provision might undermine or has undermined the efficient administration of justice. Examples of circumstances where this might arise are: i) the assistance is being provided for an improper purpose; ii) the assistance is unreasonable in nature or degree; iii) the MF is subject to a civil proceedings order or a civil restraint order; iv) the MF is using the litigant as a puppet; v) the MF is directly or indirectly conducting the litigation; vi) the court is not satisfied that the MF fully understands the duty of confidentiality.

14) Where a litigant is receiving assistance from a MF in care proceedings, the court should consider the MF's attendance at any advocates' meetings directed by the court, and, with regard to cases commenced after 1.4.08, consider directions in accordance with paragraph 13.2 of the Practice Direction Guide to Case Management in Public Law Proceedings.

15) itigants are permitted to communicate any information, including filed evidence, relating to the proceedings to MFs for the purpose of obtaining advice or assistance in relation to the proceedings.

16) Legal representatives should ensure that documents are served on litigants in good time to enable them to seek assistance regarding their content from MFs in advance of any hearing or advocates' meeting.

17) The High Court can, under its inherent jurisdiction, impose a civil restraint order on MFs who repeatedly act in ways that undermine the efficient administration of justice.

Rights of audience and rights to conduct litigation

18) MFs do **not** have a right of audience or a right to conduct litigation. It is a criminal offence to exercise rights of audience or to conduct litigation unless properly qualified and authorised to do so by an appropriate regulatory body or, in the case of an otherwise unqualified or unauthorised individual (i.e., a Lay individual including a MF), the court grants such rights on a case-by-case basis.

19) Courts should be slow to grant any application from a litigant for a right of audience or a right to conduct litigation to any Lay person, including a MF. This is because a person exercising such rights must ordinarily be properly trained, be under professional discipline (including an obligation to insure against liability for negligence) and be subject to an overriding duty to the court. These requirements are necessary for the protection of all parties to litigation and are essential to the proper administration of justice.

20) Any application for a right of audience or a right to conduct litigation to be granted to any Lay person should therefore be considered very carefully. The court should only be prepared to grant such rights where there is good reason to do so taking into account all the circumstances of the case, which are likely to vary greatly. Such grants should not be extended to Lay persons automatically or without due consideration. They should not be granted for mere convenience.

21) Examples of the type of special circumstances which have been held to justify the grant of a right of audience to a Lay person, including a MF, are: i) that person is a close relative of the litigant; ii) health problems preclude the litigant from addressing the court, or conducting litigation, and the litigant cannot afford to pay for a qualified legal representative; iii) the litigant is relatively

inarticulate and prompting by that person may unnecessarily prolong the proceedings.

22) It is for the litigant to persuade the court that the circumstances of the case are such that it is in the interests of justice for the court to grant a Lay person a right of audience or a right to conduct litigation.

23) The grant of a right of audience or a right to conduct litigation to Lay persons who hold themselves out as professional advocates or professional MFs or who seek to exercise such rights on a regular basis, whether for reward or not, will however **only** be granted in exceptional circumstances. To do otherwise would tend to subvert the will of Parliament.

24) If a litigant wants a Lay person to be granted a right of audience, an application must be made at the start of the hearing. If a right to conduct litigation is sought such an application must be made at the earliest possible time and must be made, in any event, before the Lay person does anything which amounts to the conduct of litigation. It is for litigants to persuade the court, on a case-by-case basis, that the grant of such rights is justified.

25) Rights of audience and the right to conduct litigation are separate rights. The grant of one right to a Lay person does not mean that a grant of the other right has been made. If both rights are sought their grant must be applied for individually and justified separately.

26) Having granted either a right of audience or a right to conduct litigation, the court has the power to remove either right. The grant of such rights in one set of proceedings cannot be relied on as a precedent supporting their grant in future proceedings.

Remuneration

27) Litigants can enter into lawful agreements to pay fees to MFs for the provision of reasonable assistance in court or out of court by, for instance, carrying out clerical or mechanical activities, such as photocopying documents, preparing bundles, delivering documents to opposing parties or the court, or the provision of legal advice in connection with court proceedings. Such fees cannot be lawfully recovered from the opposing party.

28) Fees said to be incurred by MFs for carrying out the conduct of litigation, where the court has not granted such a right, cannot lawfully be recovered from either the litigant for whom they carry out such work or the opposing party.

29) Fees said to be incurred by MFs for carrying out the conduct of litigation after the court has granted such a right are in principle recoverable from the litigant for whom the work is carried out. Such fees cannot be lawfully recovered from the opposing party.

30) Fees said to be incurred by MFs for exercising a right of audience following the grant of such a right by the court are in principle recoverable from the litigant on whose behalf the right is exercised. Such fees are also recoverable, in principle, from the opposing party as a recoverable disbursement: CPR 48.6(2) and 48(6)(3)(ii).

Personal Support Unit & Citizen's Advice Bureau

31) Litigants should also be aware of the services provided by local Personal Support Units and Citizens' Advice Bureaux. The PSU at the Royal Courts of Justice in London can be contacted on 020 7947 7701, by email at rcj@thepsu.org.uk, their website: www.thepsu.org.uk or at the enquiry desk. The CAB at the Royal Courts of Justice in London can be contacted on 020 7947 6564 or at the enquiry desk.

Lord Neuberger of Abbotsbury, Master of the Rolls Sir Nicholas Wall, President of the Family Division 12 July 2010

Notice of McKenzie Friend

To be completed by the Applicant/Claimant or the Respondent/Defendant

[Please fill in the form, take it to the court and hand it to the court usher before the hearing starts.]

Case Number:..

Parties: Applicant/Claimant..

Respondent/Defendant:.......................................

I am the Applicant/Claimant ( ) / Respondent/Defendant ( ) (please tick)

I wish to have a McKenzie Friend with me at the hearing. I understand that my McKenzie Friend:-

1) may provide moral support; take notes; help with case papers; quietly give advice.

2) may not address the court, make oral submissions or examine witnesses unless the

Judge gives permission;

3) in family matters, should not have an interest in the outcome of the proceedings.

The McKenzie Friend is (please tick)

(a) a relative (please give relationship) ......

(b) a friend/ neighbour/ colleague/ other (please specify) ....

(c) a free- advice agency worker ....

(d) a person I am paying to help in this case ....

If you have ticked box (c) or (d) above, please say what agency or organisation or association the person belongs to (if any).........

Name and Address of McKenzie Friend:
....
....
....
(business address if (c) or (d) above has been ticked)

The McKenzie Friend must complete below:-

1. Have you read the Practice Guidance issued on 12 July 2010 by the Head of Civil Justice and the Head of Family Justice? It is available online and displayed here http://www.judiciary.gov.uk/Resources/JCO/Documents/Guidance/mckenzie- friends-practice-guidance -july-2010.pdf
Yes / No

2. Do you agree to comply with it? Yes / No

3. Do you have a legal qualification? Yes / No If yes, please specify.................

The Judge may ask you questions about the above statements to satisfy him/herself that your answers are accurate. Those questions may be renewed at any subsequent hearing.

Signature of Litigant ....

Dated

CHAPTER 32

INSTRUCTING EXPERTS

An expert witness can be anyone with knowledge or experience of a particular field or discipline beyond that to be expected of a Lay person. The duty of the expert witness is to give the court an impartial opinion on particular aspects of matters within his/her expertise that are in dispute.

The more common experts in family proceedings are:

Paediatrician (child injury), Radiologist (fractures), Psychiatrist (capacity, alcohol, drugs), Psychologist (capacity, risk assessment), Scientists (DNA paternity), Accountants (business), Valuers (house and property), Actuaries (pensions), Social Workers (assessments).

Definition of Expert

The definition of an *'expert'* is *'a person who is very knowledgeable about or skilful in a particular area'*. This expertise means that others can have confidence that their opinion is informed and reliable. Expert witnesses are different from other witnesses who give written or spoken evidence to a court. If someone is an expert, the court is prepared to accept their opinions about a case, rather than simply evidence about what a witness has seen or heard. The duty of an expert witness is to provide independent assistance to the court through their objective, unbiased opinion about matters within their expertise. This duty is owed to the court and overrides any duty to anyone who is instructing or paying the expert.

It is the Judge's role in cases involving children, to decide what the facts are if people can't agree, and having decided the facts, to make decisions about what is in the best interests of the child. In straightforward cases, the Judge can rely on the evidence of the witness directly involved about what did or didn't happen and will not need the assistance of an expert. However, some cases are more complicated and expert evidence is necessary so that the right decision can be made for the child, for example, if a child is physically injured and no one can say how it happened or if the court needs to know more about the mental health issues facing the parents. These are areas which can only be properly understood by people who have specialised training and experience. Social workers and Children's Guardians are considered 'experts' by the court in their own area of expertise. Experts can play a role in many different types of family cases but are more common in children and financial applications.

The 'Necessary' Test:

A party must have the court's permission to instruct an expert, and this permission is only given if the party requesting the report shows that the expert report is 'necessary' to resolve proceedings justly. *Section 13(6) Children and Families Act 2014.*

The judgment of Lord Justice Munby in **Re HL [2013]** described 'necessary' evidence as being 'indispensable' as opposed just 'useful, reasonable and desirable'.

Under **Section 13(7) Children and Families Act 2014** the court must consider:

- any impact which the giving of permission would have on the welfare of the children concerned

- the issues the expert evidence would relate to

- the questions which the court would require the expert to answer

- what other expert evidence is available

- whether evidence could be given by another person on the matters on which the expert would give evidence

- the impact which giving permission would be likely to have on the case and the timetable

- the cost, and

- any matters set out in the Family Procedure Rules 2010.

The application itself

Part 25 of the Family Procedure Rules 2010 sets out the procedure that must be followed if a party seeks permission to instruct an expert.

As a general rule, an application should be made as soon as possible.

Rule 25.6 sets out when an application is to be made and **Rule 25.7** describes how it is to be made – i.e. in what form and with what supporting documents and information.

Form C2 is currently the appropriate application form to be used. There is a need to set out the field in which the expert evidence is required, identify the expert by name (if possible) so that the other parties can comment on the suitability of that particular expert. Included in the application should be a draft of the order being sought and a copy of the expert's CV, details of how long the expert will need to write a report and how much it will cost. A draft letter of instructions should be included in the papers.

The expert must have knowledge appropriate to the court case, have been active in the area of work or practice, have sufficient experience of the issues relevant to the case, be regulated or accredited to a registered body where this is appropriate, have relevant qualifications and have received appropriate training to comply with safeguarding requirements.

The Letter of Instructions

- The requirements for the letter of instruction are strict and set out in *Practice Direction 25C*. The letter of instruction should have already been drafted and attached to the application for the court's permission to instruct an expert. This should have been seen and agreed by all the parties to the case

- The expert is usually instructed by all the parties but one party will 'take the lead'. This party will be responsible for sending the letter of instruction, ensure that the expert is available to come to court and for being the first point of contact in the case of any queries. The court must approve the questions asked which must be within the ambit of the expert's area of expertise. The expert must have a list of documents, indexed and paginated. The letter of instruction must be clear as to the basis on which the expert is being instructed to provide a report and who pays the expert's fees. If the parties are paying using their own money, it is for them to enter into a contract with the expert to pay what is agreed. If the expert is to be paid by Legal Aid, care should be taken to ensure the fees are in accordance with the Legal Aid regulations.

Expert or treating professional

- An expert is appointed by, and owes a duty to, the court and thus reports in accordance with instructions from the parties.

- Treating professionals are not under the court's immediate control. They may have already produced reports that might be used in family proceedings, but probably as background material for a court appointed expert to consider.

- Therapeutic relationships and patient confidentiality should not be undermined.

- Treating professionals can be called as witnesses. If so, they are subject to the same duties to the court as an instructed expert (and should have a letter of instruction and all relevant materials).

- In family proceedings, the single joint expert is inquisitorial rather than adversarial proceedings. However, the court may allow a second expert e.g. if certain medical evidence is pivotal and difficult to challenge without a second opinion (e.g. medical imaging)

After the expert's report FPR 2010 part 25

Experts can be asked written questions within 10 days of their report but only for clarification of the report – no fee can be charged.

- Experts may be directed to attend an experts' meetings. They are required to identify the expert issues, agree on them if possible, and provide the court with a summary of what is agreed and what is not agreed.

- Experts may ask the court for directions to assist them in carrying out their functions.

Dealing with experts

- The expert should be told the hearing date as soon as possible and make time available to attend court.

- It is increasingly possible to give evidence remotely. This should be planned in advance, and links need to be tested.

- The solicitor who is instructing the expert should ensure the expert is fully updated and have the electronic bundle.

- The parties should agree as soon as possible if the expert is not needed to give evidence and inform him/her accordingly.

President's Memorandum: Experts in the Family Court

In October 2021, the President of the Family Division, Sir Andrew McFarlane, issued a President's Memorandum: Experts in the Family Court, to explain the principles applied by the court when it considers whether to authorise or admit expert evidence and as a reminder that experts should only be instructed when to do so is 'necessary' to assist the court in resolving issues justly. Expert evidence will only be 'necessary' where it is demanded by the contested issues rather than being merely reasonable, desirable or of assistance, which is a higher threshold than the standard of 'assisting the court',

The following points are also made in the Memorandum:

- that the family courts adopt a rigorous approach to the admission of expert evidence and 'pseudo-science' If this is not based on any established body of knowledge, it will be inadmissible

- to avoid delay the courts should continue to consider each application for expert instruction with care so that an application is granted only when it is necessary to do so, and

- in relation to duties to the court and professional standards, FPR 2010, PD 25B sets out the duties of the expert to the court and FPR 2010, PD 25B, para 4.1(b) requires an expert to comply with the standards set out in the annex to that Practice Direction, which includes requirements:

- to have been active in the area of work

- to have sufficient experience of the issues

- to have familiarity with the breadth of current practice or opinion, and

- if the expert's professional practice is regulated by a UK statutory body, to be in possession of a current licence, up-to-date with CPD and to have received appropriate training on the role of an expert in the family courts

https://www.judiciary.uk/wp-content/uploads/2021/10/PFD-Memo-Experts.pdf

Particular areas involving experts

Capacity

Expert evidence as to whether a party lacks capacity to conduct proceedings is likely to be necessary for the court to make a determination on the issue. In some cases the court may consider evidence from a treating clinician such as a treating psychiatrist to be sufficient. There may be fluctuations in a party's capacity to conduct the litigation over the course of the proceedings and capacity may be lost or regained during those proceedings. Expert evidence may be necessary to monitor this. Where there is concern that a party may lack capacity to conduct the proceedings, the solicitor for that party must take the lead in the instruction of an expert for the purpose of the assessment of the party's capacity to conduct the proceedings. The expert may be either the party's treating clinician or a separate expert asked to provide an opinion.

As a general rule, expert evidence in family proceedings will usually be given by a single joint expert.

Financial proceedings

As part of the disclosure process, it will often be necessary to obtain expert evidence regarding the valuation of properties, businesses and other assets (for example, jewellery, antiques or pension benefits). However, such evidence should not be obtained automatically, and although an expert may be instructed by a party in financial proceedings without the permission of the court, the court's permission must be obtained before expert evidence may put before the court in any form.

Once it is concluded that the instruction of an expert is appropriate, it is then necessary to consider whether it is appropriate to instruct a single joint expert or whether each party should instruct their own expert. Where two or more parties wish to submit expert evidence on a particular issue, 25.11 FPR 2010 permits the court to direct that evidence be given by one expert only. Wherever possible, expert evidence should be obtained from a single expert instructed by both parties. A party who wishes to instruct an expert should first give the other party a list of the names of one or more experts in the relevant speciality whom they consider suitable to be instructed.

Scientific (DNA) tests within family proceedings

Under **Part III of the Family Law Reform Act 1969**, in civil proceedings in which the parentage of any person is to be determined, the court may direct the use of scientific tests to assist in determining paternity, either of its own motion or on an application by any party to the proceedings. There is no freestanding power to direct scientific (DNA) tests and there must be civil proceedings within which the parentage issue arises.

Accredited bodies

The Ministry of Justice (MoJ) is responsible for maintaining a list of accredited bodies to carry out court-directed scientific (DNA) tests to establish parentage. The list of accredited bodies enables the court to identify the tester when it makes a direction under FLRA 1969, s 20.

Re F (children) (DNA evidence) **[2007] EWHC 3235 (Fam), [2008] 1 FLR 348 gave helpful guidance on DNA testing:**

1. an order for scientific (DNA) testing should specify that it is being made pursuant to FLRA 1969 and either the company who is to undertake the testing should be named, or the order

should direct that the company identified to undertake the testing is selected in accordance with FLRA 1969 from the MoJ accredited list—only accredited companies may be instructed

2. the taking of samples from children should only be undertaken pursuant to the express order of the court and if a need arises for further samples to be obtained, that should be arranged only with the approval of the court—if all parties agree on the need for further samples to be obtained, the application may be made in writing to the Judge who has conduct of the matter and these requirements should be communicated to the identified accredited company in the letter of instruction

3. save in cases where the issue is solely confined to paternity testing, where the accredited company may have its own standardised application form, all requests for scientific (DNA) testing should be by letter of instruction

4. the letter of instruction should emphasise that the responsibilities of DNA experts are identical to those of any expert reporting in a family case and that their overriding obligation is to the court—if any test carried out in pursuance of their instruction casts any doubt on, or appears relevant to the hypothesis set by their instructions, they should regard themselves as being under a duty to draw that to the attention of the court and the parties

5. any letter of instruction to an accredited company should set out in clear terms precisely what relationships are to be analysed and, where the information is available, the belief of the parties as to the extent of their relatedness

6. the letter of instruction should always make clear that if there appears to the expert to be any lack of clarity or ambiguity in their written instructions, or if they require further guidance,

they should revert to the solicitor instructing them and the solicitor should keep a note or memorandum of any such request

7. the reports prepared for the court by the expert should bear in mind that they are addressing Lay people and the report should strive to interpret their analysis in clear language—while it will usually be necessary to recite the tests undertaken and the likely ratios derived from them, care should be given to explain those results within the context of their identified conclusions

8. particular care should be taken in the use of phrases such as 'this result provides good evidence' as that is a relative term and such expressions should always be set within the parameters of current DNA knowledge and should identify in plain terms the limitations as to the reliability of any test carried out, a 'likelihood ratio' by definition is a concept which has uncertainty inherent within it and the extent of uncertainty will vary from test to test and the author of the report must identify and explain those parameters

9. where any particular test and subsequent ratio of likelihood is regarded as in any way controversial within the mainstream of DNA expertise, the use of the test and the reasons for its use should be signalled to the court in the report

A party to the proceedings is not entitled, unless the court otherwise directs, to call the tester, or any other person by whom any thing necessary for the purpose of enabling those tests to be carried out was done, as a witness, unless within 14 days of receipt of the report they serve notice on the other parties to the proceedings, or on such of them as the court directs, of their intention to call the tester or that other person. Where the tester is called as a witness, the party calling them is entitled to cross-examine them.

Payment for the expert

PD 25C says that the letter of instruction must be clear as to the basis on which the expert is being contracted to provide a report.

If the parties are paying using their own money, it is for them to enter into a contract with the expert to pay what is agreed.

If the expert is being paid by legal aid, solicitors should be familiar with how the Legal Aid Agency (LAA) operates.

Legal Aid

Para 1 of Schedule 5 to the Civil Legal Aid (Remuneration) Regulations 2013 provides that (**subject to paragraph 2**), the Lord Chancellor must pay the expert's costs at fixed fees, not exceeding the specified rates set out in a table. This document sets out a list of different categories of expert and the permitted maximum hourly rate for that expert.

Paragraph 2 of Schedule 5 of the 2013 Regulations sets out that an expert can be paid more than these set rates, but only if the circumstances are 'exceptional'. This is defined as meaning the evidence must be 'key' to the client's case AND either the material is so complex an expert with high level of seniority is required OR the material is so 'specialised and unusual' that only very few experts could deal with it. If parties plan that their expert is paid via the LAA, beyond these fixed rates, they have to apply to the LAA for 'prior authority' i.e. permission to go over the fixed rates. If they don't get this permission, the solicitor could end up with the bill, as they have now a contractual relationship with the expert to pay for his or her services.

The application for prior authority is via a prescribed form. If refused, there is no right of appeal.

How are costs divided between parties? And what happens if one party can't afford to pay?

The LAA will expect any joint instruction to be paid for equally by all the parties who want to rely upon the expert evidence. This can cause problems if any self representing or privately paying party says they cannot afford to pay. In care proceedings, this problem can often be side stepped by looking to the local authority and the child's solicitors to pay the fees in those cases where parents are not legally aided. Sometimes a local authority will agree to pay a shortfall in order to avoid an impasse or delay.

In private law proceedings involving two litigants in person there is no obvious route to secure an expert's instruction unless the parents pay for it themselves, and even where one party has legal aid the LAA are likely to query an order saying that they should pay both parties' share of the bill.

Further reading MoJ **'The use of experts in family law'** 2015

https://assets.publishing.service.gov.uk/government/uploads/system/uploads/attachment_data/file/486770/use-experts-family-law.pdf

CHAPTER 33

DRAFTING COURT ORDERS

Generally

A draft order is simply the wording of the written order that parties in court proceedings are asking the court to make. In cases today, family lawyers are expected to take their laptops to court and draft orders there and then. This applies to cases where at least one party is represented. Court orders are approved by the judge, drawn up and often handed to the parties on the day of the hearing. In cases involving a litigant in person, the judge or legal adviser will often draft the order. It is usually the lawyer for the applicant that takes the lead and produces a first draft. In cases where the applicant is not represented, the court will expect the lawyer for the respondent to draft the order.

Standard and Template Orders

"Inordinate amounts of time and money are spent – wasted – in the process of drafting orders that could, and therefore should, be standardised. The use of standard orders produced at the press of a button will obviate the need for drafts from counsel and solicitors scribbled out in the corridor. It should assist greatly in reducing the time judges and court staff spend approving and completing orders. And the existence of a body of standardised and judicially approved forms of order will go a long way to assisting judges and others – mediators for example – faced with the increasing number of litigants in person who cannot be expected to draft their own orders" Lord Justice Mumby

This has led to the production of a series of standardised draft court orders covering most areas of family proceedings. These orders do not have the strict status of forms within Part 5 of the FPR 2010 and their use, although very strongly to be encouraged, is not mandatory. A standard order may be varied by the court or a party if the variation is required by the circumstances of a particular case. There will be many circumstances when a variation is required and departure from the standard form will not prevent an order being valid and binding.

The prescribed order templates can be downloaded from https://www.lawsociety.org.uk/topics/family-and-children/private-law-prescribed-order-templates.

Recitals in Family Law Orders

The purpose of a recital in an order is amongst other things, to record the parties' non-binding expression of intent. Recitals are often used to cover issues that the court could not otherwise order, e.g. "neither party should criticise the other". A recital is different to a direction being recorded in the body of the order. When recorded in the body of the order the direction forms part of the order and as such, is enforceable by the court. Recitals in many family law orders are crucial in reaching an agreement. When agreeing an order, it is important to recognise when appropriate to record an agreement in a recital or the body of the order as this can have very important consequences for the parties.

President's Guidance: Forms of Orders in Children Cases was issued by Sir Andrew McFarlane, President of the Family Division, on 17 June 2019. The guidance stated that recitals in the first order and last order in any child case (public or private law) should be treated differently to recitals in any interim orders:

Paragraph 9, "the first order made in any child case (public or private law) should comply with the previous Practice Guidance or PD12B, para 14.13, so that the key information in each case is recorded there. For subsequent orders (other than final orders) the court, while following the previous Practice Guidance, should tailor the order to the particular circumstances of the case, without the need to include lengthy narrative material which does not relate to the requirements of the particular order. The minimum required content in an order following a second or subsequent interim hearing will be:

- a recital of who attended and their representation;

- a recital of the issues determined at the hearing;

- a record of any agreement or concession made during the hearing;

- a recital of the issues that remain outstanding; and

- the text of any orders that were made.

It is expected that this approach will enable the court to limit the content of orders to what is strictly required for effective case management.

Following a final hearing, the court order should, as has always been the case, set out in full the orders that the court has made, together with any appropriate recitals".

https://www.judiciary.uk/publications/president-of-the-family-divisions-guidance-forms-of-orders-in-children-cases/

As stated above, the first order should comply with PD12B para 14.13 as follows:

"Order (other than a final order) – Where no final agreement is reached, and the court is required to give case management directions, the following shall be included on the order:

- the date, time and venue of the next hearing;

- whether the author of any section 7 report is required to attend the hearing, in order to give oral evidence. A direction for the Cafcass officer or WFPO to attend court will not be made without first considering the reason why attendance is necessary, and upon what issues the Cafcass officer or WFPO will be providing evidence;

Consent Orders generally

Care should be taken in the drafting consent orders. Beware of following:

- The court has no additional powers simply because there is an agreement. Recitals may be needed as an alternative.

- The difference between recitals and orders.

- The difference between recitals and undertakings.

- What is an undertaking and how can it be enforced?

When making a financial order:

- There can be no orders against third parties.

- Orders can only be made under sections 22 to 24.

- The court has jurisdiction e.g. after decree nisi for final orders

- State the position on costs.

Consent Orders in private children cases

Parents commonly reach an agreement regarding contact and residence. but these informal agreements are not automatically legally binding and I have limited means of recourse if the opposing parent acts in breach of that informal agreement. Consent orders provide a mechanism to make an informal agreement legally binding and therefore enforceable through the family court. This informal agreement can be incorporated into a court order. It will need to be signed and dated and attached to a C100 court form. There is no legal requirement to attend mediation (MIAM) prior to applying to court for a consent order. The court will ensure that the agreement which has been reached is in the best interests of the children concerned. There will generally be a hearing which both parties will be invited to attend where the court will verify that the agreement has been reached by consent and it will be determined whether any safeguarding checks need to be conducted.

CHAPTER 34

APPEALS

Parties should be advised that they should not submit an appeal just because they do not agree with the court's decision. They are required to show they have grounds to appeal the decision made by the court.

Grounds of appeal

There is a need to show that the decision of the Judge or Lay Magistrates of the lower court was:

1. wrong, or

2. unjust because of a serious procedural or other irregularity in the Proceedings in the lower court.

There is a need to show that the Judge/Lay Magistrates did not apply the law correctly, did not follow the correct procedure, or that there are other strong reasons why the decision was wrong or unfair.

Time limits

There is a strict 21-day time limit to submit an appeal for a final order.

If this time has expired, a party can ask for permission to submit the appeal out of time. This should be set out on the Application to Appeal Form with an explanation as to why the appeal was not made within the 21-day time limit. The Judge will consider the reasons for the delay and the effect of the delay on the case.

The courts dealing with an appeal

Decisions made by Lay Magistrates or a District Judge sitting in the Family court will be heard by a Circuit Judge sitting in the Family Court.

Decisions made by a District Judge of the High Court, a Circuit Judge or Recorder in private law child proceedings will be heard by a High Court Judge sitting in the High Court.

Decisions by a District Judge (Principal Registry of Family Division) in proceedings for financial remedy will be heard by a Judge of High court Judge level sitting in the Family Court.

Decisions made by a High Court Judge sitting in the High Court, Circuit Judge or Recorder in Public Law Child Proceedings will be heard at the court of Appeal.

Permission

A party will not be required to obtain permission to submit an appeal if the decision was made by Lay Magistrates or a District Judge sitting in the Family Court. A party will be required to obtain permission if the decision was made by any other Judge. This should generally be requested orally at the hearing when the decision is made. If the Judge refuses permission to appeal, a party can seek permission to appeal from the appeal court. This request can be made in the appeal notice which is lodged with the appeal court.

Once an appeal has been submitted, the court will consider whether to grant the party permission. It can refuse permission on the basis of the application without holding a hearing. However, this will usually be where a party has exceeded the time limit to submit the appeal.

In most appeals, the parties will be informed of a date of a hearing whereby the appeal judge will look over the appeal papers submitted, hear any submissions and ask questions about the application. The judge will then decide whether the appeal has a real prospect of success or whether there is any other compelling reason why you should be given permission to appeal.

How to submit an appeal

The application to appeal is by way of an Appellant's Notice. If the appellant is appealing to the High Court he/she will need to complete the ***FP161 form***. If the appeal is to any other court, ***N161 form*** should be completed. There is a need to give reasons for the appeal, including the grounds relied on.

Costs

If an appeal fails, the appellant can be asked to pay the legal costs of the other party. This is one of the reasons why a party should be advised to be cautious about submitting an appeal.

Alternatives

If a party is unhappy with the terms of an order and wishes to change these, he/she could consider making an application for variation at a later stage.

CHAPTER 35

ENFORCEMENT OF COURT ORDERS

Enforcement of a Child Arrangements Order

An application for enforcement is made on a *Form C79*. Enforcement proceedings must be dealt with without delay and if possible, listed before the judge or lay magistrates that dealt with matters previously.

Section 11J Children Act 1989 provides:

If the court is satisfied beyond reasonable doubt that a person has failed to comply with the provisions of the Child Arrangements Order, it may make an enforcement order imposing on the person an unpaid work requirement. The court may not make an enforcement order if it is satisfied that the person had a reasonable excuse for failing to comply with the order. The burden of proof lies on the person claiming to have had a reasonable excuse, and the standard of proof is the balance of probabilities.

The court may make an enforcement order in relation to the Child Arrangements Order only on the application of a person who is, for the purposes of the Child Arrangements Order, the person with whom the child concerned lives or is to live; a person whose contact with the child concerned is provided for in the Child Arrangements Order; any individual subject to a condition under *section 11(7)(b)* or an activity condition imposed by the child arrangements order; or the child concerned.

Where the person proposing to apply for an enforcement order in relation to a Child Arrangements Order is the child concerned, the child must obtain the leave of the court before making such an application. The court may grant leave to the child concerned only if it is satisfied that he has sufficient understanding to make the proposed application. The court may suspend an enforcement order for such period as it thinks fit. The court can make more than one enforcement order in relation to the same person on the same occasion.

Matters to consider when deciding to enforce an order

Practice Direction 12B Child Arrangements Programme Paragraph 21.1 states:

When the court receives an application to enforce a Child Arrangements Order, it will consider the following:

- whether the facts for the alleged non-compliance are agreed or whether it is necessary to conduct a hearing to establish them

- the reasons for any non-compliance

- the wishes and feelings of the child

- whether any advice is required from Cafcass on the appropriate way forward

- assess and manage any risks of making further or other Child Arrangements Orders

- whether a Separated Parents Information Programme or referral for dispute resolution is appropriate

- whether an Enforcement Order may be appropriate

- the Welfare Checklist.

Penalties for Breaching a Court Order

At the top of all Child Arrangements Order there is a warning notice that sets out the consequences to both parties as to what will happen if they do not comply with the order. There are powers available to the court as set out in *Practice Direction 12B paragraph 21.6* when considering an application to enforce.

These are:

- referral of both parents to a separated parents information programme or mediation

- unpaid work requirement of between 40 and 200 hours where the court is satisfied beyond a reasonable doubt that one party has failed to comply with a provision of the Order *(Schedule A1 Section 9(2) (a-b) & Section 9(9) Children Act 1989)*

- committal to prison (in very rare/serious cases)

- changing which party the child or children live with (in very extreme/serious cases) or variation of the Child Arrangements Order to include a more defined order

- a fine

- an order for compensation for financial loss *(Section 110 Children Act 1989)*

- a Contact Enforcement Order or Suspended Enforcement Order *(Section 11J Children Act 1989)*

- a Family Assistance Order *(Section 16 Children Act 1989)*

- the court can vary a child arrangements order if it considers it to be in the best interests of the child to do so.

Breaching Spousal Maintenance Orders

If an ex-partner stops paying this maintenance, the courts have the power to enforce the order under part 33 of the Family Procedure Rules 2010 and could also order for the arrears to be paid immediately. With an enforcement, the person responsible for paying the spousal maintenance can be liable to pay the arrears and the interest on the unpaid amount of spousal maintenance. Such an action must be bought within 12 months to bring an enforcement. Where the arrears are more than 12 months, permission will be needed from the court to collect these. The court could also issue a Judgement Summons which carries a threat of imprisonment where a breach takes place.

The approach of the court in enforcement proceedings

Whether the breach is of an order regarding a child or an order in respect of money, the approach is the same: the breach has to be proved beyond reasonable doubt, and the punishment that is imposed will be partly by way of punishment and partly in order to secure compliance. The longest prison sentence that can be imposed is two years. The maximum is six weeks, where the committal is for non-payment of debt under a judgment summons.

Contempt of Court in Family Proceedings

There are **five** main categories of contempt:

- Failure to Comply with a Court Order to do an act, or not to do something, such as failure to hand over a child, failure to comply with orders to provide documents or otherwise deliberately not to follow court orders. The maximum penalty is two years imprisonment

- Publicising information about proceedings (eg about children or about private matters from family proceedings): Penalty up to two years imprisonment

- Failure to comply with a Domestic Abuse (Non-Molestation') Order where, in addition to contempt proceedings in the family courts, prosecution is by the Police or following a power of arrest attached by the court

- Contempt in the face of the court and interference with the due administration of justice (eg, calling judges 'Enemies of the People', or discouraging your opponent from pursuing their case)

- Judgement Summons. Failure to pay sums of money where the maximum penalty is 6 weeks imprisonment. The Judgment Summons procedure which is still available in family courts under Section 5 Debtors Act 1869. This applies where money is said not to have been paid, but it is rarely used by the courts as a means of enforcement because other newer methods are available and more effective.

CHAPTER 36

THIRTY-THREE COMMON QUESTIONS ASKED BY CLIENTS IN FAMILY CASES

Divorce

1. Question: I understand that the divorce law has changed recently. Are the grounds for divorce the same as before?

Answer: Until 6th April 2022 a party seeking divorce had to satisfy the court that the legal test of irretrievable breakdown was met, by citing one or more of 'five factors': unreasonable behaviour, adultery, or desertion. separation for two years with consent and five years separation. The Divorce, Dissolution and Separation Act 2020 has reformed the law on divorce from 6th April 2022 by removing the requirement to provide evidence of 'conduct' or 'separation' and replacing it with a simple requirement to provide a statement of irretrievable breakdown of the marriage or civil partnership, or to obtain a judicial separation. The new law has also removed the ability to defend the decision to divorce or end the civil partnership. It also allows for the first time, joint applications for divorce, dissolution, and separation, meaning that couples can now apply together.

2. Question: How long does it take to be divorced?

Answer: The new law has introduced a new minimum overall time frame of six months (26 weeks) made up of a 'minimum period' of twenty weeks in divorce proceedings between the start of proceedings and when the applicant may apply for a conditional order. The current minimum time period between the conditional order and final order is six weeks. This ensures that there is a period of reflection and provides an opportunity for couples to agree the practical arrangements for the future.3. Question: How much does it cost to be divorced?

Answer: With the procedure itself being streamlined and the majority of divorces being processed on line, one would expect the cost of the divorce to be reduced in time. The court fee is £593. Solicitors have been charging fees in the region of £750–1000 plus the court fees, but much will depend on the law firm involved.

4. Question: Is the terminology the same since the divorce law has changed?

Answer: There have been a number of changes in terminology:

'Petition' has become 'Application', 'Petitioner' has become 'Applicant', 'Decree Nisi' has become 'Conditional Order' and 'Decree Absolute' has become 'Final Order'. This makes the language simpler and is intended to be more accessible to the general public.

5. Question: What documents are needed to commence divorce proceedings?

Answer: The original marriage certificate or a certified copy, the divorce application (known as Form D8) and the court fee.

6. Question: Does it matter who starts the divorce?

Answer: No. A divorce application can be filed individually or jointly with your spouse.

7. Question: When am I considered divorced?

Answer: On the granting of the Final Order previously known as the Decree Absolute

CHAPTER 36

Cohabitation

8. Question: What is a common law marriage?

Answer: There is no such thing.

9. Question: What if my partner leaves and stops paying the bills?

Answer: This depends on whether the bills are in joint names, in your name or your partner's name that has left. In joint names you will be both individually and jointly liable for the outstanding debts. If it is in your partners name he or she will be liable.

10. Question: We are not married and we live in my partner's home. Am I entitled to anything?

Answer: There is no simple answer to this. The law gives no automatic rights to a partner in these circumstances, but if you contributed towards the deposit on a purchase or have provided money for significant improvement to the house, you may have a claim. It is important that the details are considered carefully.

11. Question: What if my partner will not leave our shared property?

Answer: If you have not entered into an agreement as to how long you are going to live together and separate, then when coming to separate and leaving a property that will depend on how the property is owned or rented. If it is in joint names, then it may be hard in the short term to enforce someone to leave the property. In the long term, you may need the court's assistance. Careful consideration of the options available is required. It can depend on whether there is a threat of violence itself and if there are children at the property.

12. Question: If we have been living together, but have not married, does everything have to be split 50/50?

Answer: Not necessarily. If you have decided something about the house you live in or property you own and that has been recorded on the deeds, then it has to be followed. However, it can sometimes be challenged. If not, there are different areas of law that govern this subject and it can depend on your circumstances. It is possible that someone ends up with nothing.

Private Children cases

13. Question: What is parental responsibility?

Answer: There is no legal definition of parental responsibility. it includes the rights and responsibility to make welfare decisions for a child such as education, health, religion, where are child lives. However, this is not an extensive list.

14. Question: How do I gain parental responsibility?

Answer: A mother obtains parental responsibility by giving birth. A father, however, has this responsibility only if he is married to the mother when the child is born or has acquired legal responsibility for the child through one of the following three routes:

- Jointly registering the birth of the child with the mother
- A parental responsibility agreement with the mother
- A parental responsibility order made by the court

15. Question: What is custody and access?

Answer: These terms are not terms now recognised by the family court in England and Wales. We have referred to residence and contact but even more recently these terms have been overtaken by expressions under a Child Arrangements order.

16. Question: What happens to the children if we are split up and we are not married?

Answer: It does not make any difference if you are married or not. The important things are to have parental responsibility and to consider the children welfare needs.

17. Question: Can you stop a violent ex-partner from seeing his child?

Answer: After the implementation of the Children and Families Act 2014 there is a presumption that contact with both parents is in the best interests of the child. Although a parent could stop contact with a violent ex-partner, they cannot stop them applying to the court for a Child Arrangements Order to facilitate contact with their child. If an application was made the court would have to decide if it is suitable to allow contact with the ex-partner. It does not always follow that because they were a violent partner they were a violent parent.

18. Question: Can I move abroad with my children?

Answer: You cannot move children out of the country without the other parent's consent. The first step is to try to obtain the other parent's consent to the move. If consent cannot be obtained voluntarily an application has to be made to the court for 'permission to remove from the jurisdiction'.

19. Question: Will child maintenance payments stop if I remarry?

Answer: Child maintenance is a payment made by an absent parent for their child. Payments are not made for the ex-partner and as such your relationship status has no bearing on the continuance of the payments. An absent parent has an ongoing legal obligation to maintain their child until they attain the age of 18.

20. Question: How much child maintenance should I pay?

Answer: This area is governed by statute and the easiest way to find out how much you are liable to pay is to look up the Child Maintenance Service website.

Finances and Property matters following divorce

21. Question: How do financial divorce settlements work?

Answer: A financial settlement is the agreement you reach with your former partner regarding the division of your money, property and other assets. The courts set the details of this agreement and make it a binding financial order. When the courts draw up financial settlements, they take certain key factors into consideration. Chief among these are the arrangements for any children of the marriage. In particular, the court will want to know where they will live in future so their housing needs can be properly assessed. Another major factor will be the length of the marriage. The longer it lasted, the greater the settlement the court will order. Generally speaking, marriages which have lasted less than five years are considered short; those that have lasted more than fourteen years would be considered longer marriages. An additional important consideration is the specifics of each party's finances. Each half of the couple will need to fill in a signed statement called a Form E which sets out their future income and financial needs.

22. Question: How much spousal maintenance will I have to pay?

Answer: There is no set formula for calculating spousal maintenance. There are a number of factors which contribute towards the calculation of spousal maintenance including needs and affordability. Maintenance can always be varied upwards and downwards as circumstances change eg the paying party is made redundant. Maintenance comes to an end automatically if the person receiving receiving it remarries. It does not come to an end automatically if the person receiving maintenance starts to cohabit unless the final order in the financial proceedings provides for that eventuality.

23. Question: How long will I have to pay maintenance for in divorce proceedings?

Answer: In relation to children, an absent parent should broadly regard themselves as being liable until the child has concluded full time education. Spousal maintenance duration will depend upon the length of the marriage and whether or not there are dependent. For example, if the marriage is short and there are no children, the likelihood is that no maintenance will be payable or only payable for a short time. The court has a duty to consider whether a clean break is appropriate and if so, when this can be achieved without undue hardship.

24. Question: What is the position regarding pensions following divorce?

Answer: Pensions are an important part of a financial settlement. Pensions are likely to be a significant issue if the marriage is long and /or there are children of the relationship. Pensions will be less important if the marriage is short, there are no children and/or the parties are relatively young.

25. Question: Is it always a 50/50 division of assets following divorce?

Answer: The starting point is usually 50/50 but the court has a check list of factors to consider whether equality would be a fair outcome. If there are dependent children housing them will be the most influential factor.

26. Question: Are prenuptial agreements legally binding?

Answer: Recent case law asserts that the likelihood is a properly drafted agreement entered into in appropriate circumstances will be upheld in a future divorce. Tailored advice is imperative on the subject in order to obtain the most effective result.

Domestic Abuse

27. Question: Can I get my partner removed from the house if (s)he is violent?

Answer: It depends on the facts but no-one can be expected to live in the same house as a violent partner. The courts will always be open to protect a victim from a violent partner. Urgent applications can be made to the court to stop a violent partner behaving badly and orders can be made to remove the person concerned from the house where you live. This is, of course, in addition to assistance you can receive from the police and the criminal courts by way of bail conditions.

28. Question: What protection is available to me if my partner is seriously abusive towards me?

Answer: A non-molestation order and an occupation order is available. Once again it depends on the facts. Both orders can involve the perpetrator being arrested by the police should there be any breach of the order.

Public Children Law Cases – Care proceedings

29. Question: Can the local Authority remove my child without a court order?

Answer: No, the Local Authority cannot remove a child from your care unless you consent to this (usually in writing) or obtains a court order. Even if you consent to the removal, you can withdraw your consent, forcing the LA to obtain a court order.

30. Question: What does the local Authority have to show in order to obtain a court order to remove my child?

Answer: The court can make a number of court orders to remove a child from your care:

1. **Emergency Protection Order** where the court must be satisfied that the child is at risk of or is suffering harm. An EPO will last for a period of 8 days although the LA can apply for an extension to that time. This order can be made in the absence of the parent.

2. **Interim Care Order** is a temporary order and lasts up to 8 weeks at first, but can be extended. The court must have **reasonable grounds** to believe that the child has suffered or is at risk of suffering significant harm as a result of the care provided by the parents.

3. **Final Care Order** the court the court must be satisfied that the child is suffering or is likely to suffer significant harm and the likelihood of harm is attributable to the care provided by the parent. The future care of the child will be decided on what's best for the child.

32. Question: If my child is removed from my care under a court order, do I have the right to have regular contact?

Answer: Yes, the LA have a duty to promote contact between the parent and the child unless there is good reason for not doing so. The level of contact and arrangements will be agreed with the LA. A parent can apply to the court if she/he is not satisfied with the LA's proposals of contact.

33. Question: Will an adoption order be made automatically if a final care order is made?

Answer: No, the parents can consent to an adoption order. If they object, the LA will have to prove that the parents are 'withholding their consent unreasonably'.

MORE BOOKS BY LAW BRIEF PUBLISHING

A selection of our other titles available now:-

'A Practical Guide to Estate Administration and Crypto Assets' by Richard Marshall
'A Practical Guide to Managing GDPR Data Subject Access Requests – Second Edition' by Patrick O'Kane
'A Practical Guide to Parental Alienation in Private and Public Law Children Cases' by Sam King QC & Frankie Shama
'Contested Heritage – Removing Art from Land and Historic Buildings' by Richard Harwood QC, Catherine Dobson, David Sawtell
'The Limits of Separate Legal Personality: When Those Running a Company Can Be Held Personally Liable for Losses Caused to Third Parties Outside of the Company' by Dr Mike Wilkinson
'A Practical Guide to Transgender Law' by Robin Moira White & Nicola Newbegin
'Artificial Intelligence – The Practical Legal Issues (2nd Edition)' by John Buyers
'A Practical Guide to Residential Freehold Conveyancing' by Lorraine Richardson
'A Practical Guide to Pensions on Divorce for Lawyers' by Bryan Scant
'A Practical Guide to Challenging Sham Marriage Allegations in Immigration Law' by Priya Solanki
'A Practical Guide to Legal Rights in Scotland' by Sarah-Jane Macdonald
'A Practical Guide to New Build Conveyancing' by Paul Sams & Rebecca East
'A Practical Guide to Defending Barristers in Disciplinary Cases' by Marc Beaumont
'A Practical Guide to Inherited Wealth on Divorce' by Hayley Trim
'A Practical Guide to Practice Direction 12J and Domestic Abuse in Private Law Children Proceedings' by Rebecca Cross & Malvika Jaganmohan
'A Practical Guide to Confiscation and Restraint' by Narita Bahra QC, John Carl Townsend, David Winch
'A Practical Guide to the Law of Forests in Scotland' by Philip Buchan
'A Practical Guide to Health and Medical Cases in Immigration Law' by Rebecca Chapman & Miranda Butler

'A Practical Guide to Bad Character Evidence for Criminal Practitioners' by Aparna Rao
'A Practical Guide to Extradition Law post-Brexit' by Myles Grandison et al
'A Practical Guide to Hoarding and Mental Health for Housing Lawyers' by Rachel Coyle
'A Practical Guide to Psychiatric Claims in Personal Injury – 2nd Edition' by Liam Ryan
'Stephens on Contractual Indemnities' by Richard Stephens
'A Practical Guide to the EU Succession Regulation' by Richard Frimston
'A Practical Guide to Solicitor and Client Costs – 2nd Edition' by Robin Dunne
'Constructive Dismissal – Practice Pointers and Principles' by Benjimin Burgher
'A Practical Guide to Religion and Belief Discrimination Claims in the Workplace' by Kashif Ali
'A Practical Guide to the Law of Medical Treatment Decisions' by Ben Troke
'Fundamental Dishonesty and QOCS in Personal Injury Proceedings: Law and Practice' by Jake Rowley
'A Practical Guide to the Law in Relation to School Exclusions' by Charlotte Hadfield & Alice de Coverley
'A Practical Guide to Divorce for the Silver Separators' by Karin Walker
'The Right to be Forgotten – The Law and Practical Issues' by Melissa Stock
'A Practical Guide to Planning Law and Rights of Way in National Parks, the Broads and AONBs' by James Maurici QC, James Neill et al
'A Practical Guide to Election Law' by Tom Tabori
'A Practical Guide to the Law in Relation to Surrogacy' by Andrew Powell
'A Practical Guide to Claims Arising from Fatal Accidents – 2nd Edition' by James Patience
'A Practical Guide to the Ownership of Employee Inventions – From Entitlement to Compensation' by James Tumbridge & Ashley Roughton
'A Practical Guide to Asbestos Claims' by Jonathan Owen & Gareth McAloon
'A Practical Guide to Stamp Duty Land Tax in England and Northern Ireland' by Suzanne O'Hara
'A Practical Guide to the Law of Farming Partnerships' by Philip Whitcomb
'Covid-19, Homeworking and the Law – The Essential Guide to Employment and GDPR Issues' by Forbes Solicitors
'Covid-19 and Criminal Law – The Essential Guide' by Ramya Nagesh

'Covid-19 and Family Law in England and Wales – The Essential Guide' by Safda Mahmood
'A Practical Guide to the Law of Unlawful Eviction and Harassment – 2nd Edition' by Stephanie Lovegrove
'Covid-19, Brexit and the Law of Commercial Leases – The Essential Guide' by Mark Shelton
'A Practical Guide to Costs in Personal Injury Claims – 2nd Edition' by Matthew Hoe
'A Practical Guide to the General Data Protection Regulation (GDPR) – 2nd Edition' by Keith Markham
'Ellis on Credit Hire – Sixth Edition' by Aidan Ellis & Tim Kevan
'A Practical Guide to Working with Litigants in Person and McKenzie Friends in Family Cases' by Stuart Barlow
'Protecting Unregistered Brands: A Practical Guide to the Law of Passing Off' by Lorna Brazell
'A Practical Guide to Secondary Liability and Joint Enterprise Post-Jogee' by Joanne Cecil & James Mehigan
'A Practical Guide to the Pre-Action RTA Claims Protocol for Personal Injury Lawyers' by Antonia Ford
'A Practical Guide to Neighbour Disputes and the Law' by Alexander Walsh
'A Practical Guide to Forfeiture of Leases' by Mark Shelton
'A Practical Guide to Coercive Control for Legal Practitioners and Victims' by Rachel Horman
'A Practical Guide to Rights Over Airspace and Subsoil' by Daniel Gatty
'Tackling Disclosure in the Criminal Courts – A Practitioner's Guide' by Narita Bahra QC & Don Ramble
'A Practical Guide to the Law of Driverless Cars – Second Edition' by Alex Glassbrook, Emma Northey & Scarlett Milligan
'A Practical Guide to TOLATA Claims' by Greg Williams
'A Practical Guide to Elderly Law – 2nd Edition' by Justin Patten
'A Practical Guide to Responding to Housing Disrepair and Unfitness Claims' by Iain Wightwick
'A Practical Guide to the Construction and Rectification of Wills and Trust Instruments' by Edward Hewitt
'A Practical Guide to the Law of Bullying and Harassment in the Workplace' by Philip Hyland

'How to Be a Freelance Solicitor: A Practical Guide to the SRA-Regulated Freelance Solicitor Model' by Paul Bennett
'A Practical Guide to Prison Injury Claims' by Malcolm Johnson
'A Practical Guide to the Small Claims Track - 2nd Edition' by Dominic Bright
'A Practical Guide to Advising Clients at the Police Station' by Colin Stephen McKeown-Beaumont
'A Practical Guide to Antisocial Behaviour Injunctions' by Iain Wightwick
'Practical Mediation: A Guide for Mediators, Advocates, Advisers, Lawyers, and Students in Civil, Commercial, Business, Property, Workplace, and Employment Cases' by Jonathan Dingle with John Sephton
'The Mini-Pupillage Workbook' by David Boyle
'A Practical Guide to Crofting Law' by Brian Inkster
'A Practical Guide to Spousal Maintenance' by Liz Cowell
'A Practical Guide to the Law of Domain Names and Cybersquatting' by Andrew Clemson
'A Practical Guide to the Law of Gender Pay Gap Reporting' by Harini Iyengar
'NHS Whistleblowing and the Law' by Joseph England
'Employment Law and the Gig Economy' by Nigel Mackay & Annie Powell
'A Practical Guide to Noise Induced Hearing Loss (NIHL) Claims' by Andrew Mckie, Ian Skeate, Gareth McAloon
'An Introduction to Beauty Negligence Claims – A Practical Guide for the Personal Injury Practitioner' by Greg Almond
'Intercompany Agreements for Transfer Pricing Compliance' by Paul Sutton
'Zen and the Art of Mediation' by Martin Plowman
'A Practical Guide to the SRA Principles, Individual and Law Firm Codes of Conduct 2019 – What Every Law Firm Needs to Know' by Paul Bennett
'A Practical Guide to Adoption for Family Lawyers' by Graham Pegg
'A Practical Guide to Industrial Disease Claims' by Andrew Mckie & Ian Skeate
'A Practical Guide to Redundancy' by Philip Hyland
'A Practical Guide to Vicarious Liability' by Mariel Irvine
'A Practical Guide to Applications for Landlord's Consent and Variation of Leases' by Mark Shelton
'A Practical Guide to Relief from Sanctions Post-Mitchell and Denton' by Peter Causton

'A Practical Guide to Equity Release for Advisors' by Paul Sams
'A Practical Guide to Financial Services Claims' by Chris Hegarty
'The Law of Houses in Multiple Occupation: A Practical Guide to HMO Proceedings' by Julian Hunt
'Occupiers, Highways and Defective Premises Claims: A Practical Guide Post-Jackson – 2nd Edition' by Andrew Mckie
'A Practical Guide to Financial Ombudsman Service Claims' by Adam Temple & Robert Scrivenor
'A Practical Guide to Advising Schools on Employment Law' by Jonathan Holden
'A Practical Guide to Running Housing Disrepair and Cavity Wall Claims: 2nd Edition' by Andrew Mckie & Ian Skeate
'A Practical Guide to Holiday Sickness Claims – 2nd Edition' by Andrew Mckie & Ian Skeate
'Arguments and Tactics for Personal Injury and Clinical Negligence Claims' by Dorian Williams
'A Practical Guide to Drone Law' by Rufus Ballaster, Andrew Firman, Eleanor Clot
'A Practical Guide to Compliance for Personal Injury Firms Working With Claims Management Companies' by Paul Bennett
'RTA Allegations of Fraud in a Post-Jackson Era: The Handbook – 2nd Edition' by Andrew Mckie
'RTA Personal Injury Claims: A Practical Guide Post-Jackson' by Andrew Mckie
'On Experts: CPR35 for Lawyers and Experts' by David Boyle
'An Introduction to Personal Injury Law' by David Boyle

These books and more are available to order online direct from the publisher at www.lawbriefpublishing.com, where you can also read free sample chapters. For any queries, contact us on 0844 587 2383 or mail@lawbriefpublishing.com.

Our books are also usually in stock at www.amazon.co.uk with free next day delivery for Prime members, and at good legal bookshops such as Wildy & Sons.

We are regularly launching new books in our series of practical day-to-day practitioners' guides. Visit our website and join our free newsletter to be kept informed and to receive special offers, free chapters, etc.

You can also follow us on Twitter at www.twitter.com/lawbriefpub.

Printed in Dunstable, United Kingdom

66056723R00152